COWPASTURE

By the same author:
Wanderlust
Atomic Challenge

DAVID & CHARLES
Newton Abbot   London   North Pomfret (Vt)

COWPASTURE

The everyday life of an English allotment

ROY LACEY
Illustrated by Jan Martin

British Library Cataloguing in Publication Data

Lacey, Roy
  Cowpasture.
  1. Gardening
  I. Title
  635   SB453

  ISBN 0–7153–7916–X

Library of Congress Catalog Card Number: 79–56041

Typeset by
Northern Phototypesetting Co., Bolton
Printed in Great Britain
by A. Wheaton & Co., Limited Exeter
for David & Charles (Publishers) Limited
Brunel House Newton Abbot Devon

Published in the United States of America
by David & Charles Inc
North Pomfret Vermont 05053 USA

CONTENTS

For Margaret, the cook of the plot

Cowpasture and its people are as real as the book you are holding, but some names have been changed to lessen the risk of damaging friendships that are still growing.

R.L.

1

SET LIKE A JEWEL

Seventy or so miles north from London and easterly, the sky grows larger, the earth flatter, the towns smaller, the air fresher. This is East Anglia, a region still dominated by the gifts of the sea on the one side and the needs and the bounty of the soil on the other.

In southern parts of the region there are orchards, strawberry fields and villages with Norman names. Then the great midland belt of arable farms – the granary of Britain – now almost treeless and hedgeless except in the hamlets where there are still tree-lined churchyards, thatched roofs and pink-washed walls. The market towns are swamped by cars and lorries, and the few arterial roads carry an endless stream of juggernauts to and from the Haven Ports. But East Anglia retains its indefinable character.

Critics stress the dullness, the lack of surprise in the landscape. And this is so until you remember Constable country, the Deben, Orwell and Stour estuaries, Waveney valley, the Broads, Breckland, Thetford Chase and the lonely loveliness of much of the Suffolk and Norfolk coastline.

The northerner, used to the third dimension of moors and mountains, could never be truly content with this eastern plateau. Or, perhaps, its people, traditionally insular countryfolk who accept the searching misery of the east wind with dourness, are too often over-suspicious of strangers. But to those who fall in love with East Anglia its faults can be forgiven.

Certainly, for me, there is no place on earth where I would rather spend most of my time than the plot of land I cultivate in Suffolk, which is part of the allotments area called Cowpasture on the edge of Felixstowe.

Seen from the air, Cowpasture is set with jewel-like precision in the landscape. At ground level that landscape has a charm that never fails, whatever the season or time of day, to enrapture me. To the east is a field of about 6 acres used for growing barley and sugar beet and, in the days when the farmer kept pigs, kale. Beyond that is the Grove, a half-mile-long sliver of woodland that we, in the old part of Felixstowe, count as one of our most important possessions. The Grove is a superb backcloth, a middle-distant feature from the centre of Cowpasture.

Northwards, beyond the allotments' boundary hedge, is farmland, the large unfolding fields of Cowpasture Farm, with a scattering of cottages and a lane winding among them. Farther still is the wide beauty of the Deben estuary, sprinkled with slow-moving sails in the summer, flecked with gulls and lit by the crystal-clear light from the great bowl of the Suffolk sky. Tucked into this distant view is the tower of Ramsholt church, four miles away and, a mite nearer, the Ramsholt Arms pub at the waterside.

Westward are the farmhouse and barns of Cowpasture Farm, and a coppice hiding the sight, but not the sound, of wild duck on Gulpher pond. Beyond are the villages of Kirton and Falkenham, Bucklesham and Newbourn.

Felixstowe is to the south. The nearest homes are bungalows for pensioners, only 200 yards away across a new road cut as a by-pass to carry the ever-growing docks traffic.

The farms on this fertile peninsula have ancient names: Cowpasture itself, Laurel, Candlet, Searsons, Gulpher, Eastend. Modern farming techniques have destroyed many of the farms' individual personalities, particularly the hedgerows, and Dutch elm disease is taking a terrible toll of the county's most widespread tree species.

Possibly the worst feature of this part of Suffolk is an alien one – the American presence. The United States Air Force occupies two large bases at Bentwaters and Woodbridge, only six miles away as the jet flies. They have been there since 1941 when they were bomber bases. Now there are jet strike aircraft and enormous helicopters, so the pollution of the airspace is ear-shattering and seemingly unchecked. We tend to have a very jaundiced view about our role as an aircraft-carrier crewed by the USAF.

Cowpasture plots are not the only allotments in Felixstowe, but it is the largest site, serving Old Felixstowe and adjacent Walton. The original Cowpasture allotments site was bought by Felixstowe UDC in 1937 from South County Freeholds, a development company. It measured 835ft by 720ft by 500ft, covered 11.957 acres, and cost the council £4,000. It was then in use as allotments and had been for about forty years. They were let by the landlord, South County Freeholds, from 1932 to 1937, and before 1932 by Capt E. G. Prettyman. Prettyman owned an enormous area of Felixstowe, including Cowpasture Farm and hundreds of acres at the mouth of the Orwell. The latter are now the Port of Felixstowe, one of the most modern in Europe and the fastest-growing port in Britain.

The Cowpasture site grew in 1971 when the council bought two parcels of land, bordering the spur to the new by-pass for the docks, from Cyril Wiseman. So the original 185 plots became 200, varying in size from 5 rods (150sq yd) to 20 rods (600sq yd).

Twelve years ago only three out of four plots were cultivated: in 1965 there were eighty-five vacant plots out of the town's total of 341, and the council had the empty plots and headlands ploughed in spring to stop weed-seeding. Now there is a waiting list, and as 20-rod plots become vacant through the death or infirmity of the older tenants, so they are split into 10- and 5-rod plots.

In earlier days one went to the plots on foot or by cycle. Now the council has laid down a hard standing to park twenty or so

11

cars, and one sunny day in June forty-seven cars were parked on and around the site. It is no surprise today to find the doctor digging alongside the bank manager among the pensioners.

Responsibility for letting the plots rests with the town clerk, while allotment policy is decided by the town council's quaintly named Other Purposes Committee, formerly the Parks and Recreation Committee. Before World War II annual rents were 2s 6d (12½p) for a 10-rod plot. After the war this went up to 5s (25p), then 7s 6d (37½p). In October 1975, during the government's pay restraint policy to fight inflation, rents were increased by 150 per cent from 4p a rod to 10p a rod. This, understandably, caused a lot of anger among the pensioner tenants. Since then the landlord–tenant relationship has worsened.

Successive Whitehall orders to councils to prune costs have meant that our council no longer cuts the allotment paths and headlands – it hasn't the manpower to do it or the cash to employ a contractor. But, as landlord, the council tends to be too easy on those tenants who take on a plot in a flush of enthusiasm and then cultivate only a part of it. As a result Cowpasture is dotted with areas of uncultivated plots giving cover to rabbits and rats and breeding ground for nettles and thistles.

Each tenant signs an agreement with the council which stipulates that the rent shall be paid in advance on 11 October each year of the tenancy. It also warns the tenant to comply with the following conditions:

> He shall keep the allotment garden clean and in a good state of cultivation and fertility and fully cropped and free from weeds and in good condition . . .
> He shall not cause, permit or suffer any nuisance or annoyance to the occupier of any other allotment garden or to the owner or occupier of any adjoining land or obstruct any road or path . . .
> He shall not underlet, assign or part with possession of the allotment garden without the written consent of the Committee.
> He shall not without the written consent of the Committee take, sell or carry away any mineral, gravel, sand or clay.

He shall keep all ditches properly cleansed and all hedges neatly clipped or trimmed and all roads and paths clear of weeds and rubbish . . .

He shall not without written consent cause, permit or suffer any building, structure or erection to be erected or placed on the allotment garden or on any road or path . . .

He shall not use barbed wire for a fence . . .

Subject to him obtaining the prior consent of the Committee, the tenant shall be permitted to keep pigs or fowls or other livestock on the allotment garden but the amount of land to be used for such a purpose shall not exceed 25 per cent of the total area . . .

Subject to prior consent etc, he shall be permitted to erect a small hut for the storage of tools . . .

And finally there is a warning that the tenancy may be terminated:

If the rent is in arrears for not less than 40 days, or

If the tenant is not duly observing, performing, fulfilling and keeping the conditions of his tenancy, or

If he becomes bankrupt or compounds with his creditors.

The tenancy 'may also be terminated by the Committee or the tenant by not less than 12 months' notice in writing'. But this is very seldom done.

The town clerk told me, 'I try to be fair and considerate to tenants who don't keep their plots cultivated. In most cases it is due to illness, an operation perhaps. Sometimes I have to send a letter reminding a tenant of his obligations to keep the plot tidy, but it is only recently that we have had to give people notice to quit, just a few.'

The Germans have the *wunderbar* idea of making their allotments into country retreats for city dwellers. The German allotment tenant pays a rent of about 1p a square yard. For this he has the right to build a chalet up to 270sq ft on his plot and can live there at weekends and holidays. The site frequently has well-maintained roads, club rooms, including a restaurant, bars and a garden centre.

In Scotland they call them garden allotments. Rents average 1p a square yard and some local authorities have landscaped the sites and provided standard greenhouses and huts. Glasgow has a plan for leisure gardens – allotments with a rest garden, play area for young children and some landscaping with lawns and trees.

The contrast with Cowpasture is extreme. 'We provide nothing but the plot itself,' said the town clerk, 'not even a water supply.' But to many of us at Cowpasture a stake in this beautifully sited piece of Suffolk is enough. The Germans and the Scots can have their leisure gardens planned and laid out for them. For all its faults, I prefer the benign landlordship of our council.

2

THE BEST ASSET
FOR A FAMILY

Many of Britain's allotment gardens are the most fertile and productive pieces of land in the country. Older sites may have been in continuous use for hundreds of years, and generations of gardeners have farmed them, mucked them and passed them on that much better than when they took them over.

Monks were probably the earliest allotment holders. There are records dating back to 1200 showing that at the monasteries monks were allowed their own plots for cultivating herbs and vegetables. The Romans established traditions and techniques of gardening along with varieties of fruit and vegetables which were the forerunners of today's varieties. They grew cabbages, peas, beans, turnips, carrots, parsnips, beetroots, radishes, asparagus, onions, lettuces, chicory, garlic and endive. They had heated greenhouses and at least twenty-two varieties of apples, thirty-six of pears, and eight of cherries. When they left Britain their skills as gardeners remained for the monasteries, universities and noblemen's estates to perpetuate.

Lords of the manor doled out pieces of land for their serfs to cultivate, taking fresh fruit and vegetables as rent. After the Enclosures, private landowners would let parcels of land for use by villagers, and at Melbourne, in Derbyshire, land was set aside as allotments for poor villagers, with the conditions that the tenants must only use a spade for cultivation and must not work on the plots on Sundays.

The Allotments Act of 1887 gave local councils power to acquire land by compulsory purchase for allotment gardens, and these powers were extended by the Small Holdings and Allotments Act of 1908. The Allotments Act of 1922 was the major statute. It appeared after World War I had shown how dependent Britain is on home-grown supplies of food and how big a contribution the allotment holder can make.

This Act compelled all local councils administering areas with a population of 10,000 or more to set up an allotments committee for the purposes of acquiring land for letting to tenants and generally applying the council's allotment gardens policy. It also made a legal distinction between allotments and allotment gardens. An allotment garden is a plot of not more than 40 poles (1,210sq yd) in area which is wholly or mainly cultivated by the occupier for the production of fruit and vegetable crops for consumption by himself or his family. An allotment is any parcel of land of not more than 2 acres if privately owned, or not more than 5 acres if provided by a local authority, which is cultivated as a farm or garden or both. Model rules for the administration of plots were incorporated in the various Acts.

In 1939 the Cultivation of Lands (Allotments) Order paved the way for the 'Dig for Victory' campaign by giving town halls much wider powers. They could now take over any occupied land which could conveniently be cultivated, on payment of a rent or compensation or both. Common land, village greens and public parks in towns and cities could all be requisitioned for wartime allotments. The contribution these allotments made to wartime self-sufficiency was massive. Together with vegetable production from private gardens, possibly as much as one-half of all the vegetables consumed in the United Kingdom were home-grown in this way.

The parks reverted to their normal use after 1945, and there was a general rundown of allotment gardens until the 1970s when inflation hit family budgets harder and harder. Now there are at least 120,000 people waiting for allotments. In

England and Wales the total number of plots is about 500,000 compared with three times that number at the height of the 1939-45 War.

If we had the same spirit of urgency now as we had then, the waiting list for plots would disappear almost overnight. There are more than 100,000 acres of derelict land in England alone, most of it owned by British Rail and the Ministry of Defence. These unused acres would break down into at least 1,500,000 allotment plots which would still be productive a long time after the last drop of North Sea oil has been burned. But ours is not a rational democracy. Rather than turn land to the production of food, we allow motorways to swallow up 70,000 acres of farmland a year, and even more disappear under concrete for industrial and residential development.

Inflation has been a prime mover in this rush for plots of gold. As the director of the Henry Doubleday Research Association, Mr Lawrence Hills, noted, 'The best asset for any family is a profitable allotment.' People do not want allotments just to grow their own better-flavoured, cheaper vegetables and fruit. There is today, among those embroiled in this highly competitive and strongly materialistic society, a deep wish to get back to the fundamentals of the soil, fresh air, the sun, rain and the sweat of the brow. As an allotment holder you can make your own small but important protest against this plastic age of take-away tastelessness and convenience foods.

The allotment garden has not, to my knowledge, spread to the United States. Dieticians there are concerned at the effects of too much reliance on convenience foods and especially the packaged take-away 'whole' meals. These are rich in carbohydrates but so lacking in vitamins and trace elements that there is now the American phenomenon of a nation of obese citizens suffering from malnutrition.

Take-away meals are displacing our traditional fish and chip shops and offering, nutritionally, not something better, but something far worse. The publicity tells us they fulfil a need, but I believe it is a need that the firms created themselves.

Looking back, I do not recall anyone crying to the moon for a piece of over-spiced chicken before the advent of the finger-lickin'-good craze.

Life loses its interest when there is nothing to look forward to. Though the gardener at times may feel desperate, he seldom feels suicidal, because tomorrow it is bound to rain and break the drought or stop raining so that sowing can commence. The seasons and their role in the gardening cycle have added attractions when you are growing your own food, and even in the doldrum days of deepest winter you can sit and plan to meet the needs of your family from the capabilities of your plot. And you can gear your effort, changing up or down, according to age and the time available for farming the allotment.

Maximum effort, with all four cylinders firing smoothly, is the prerogative of the healthy young husband when a growing family is making maximum demand on the output from the plot. After that there can be a more restrained cruising period when quality rather than quantity and an eye on the show bench are dominant. By then allotment gardening will have become a way of life with deep satisfactions that hold as good in retirement as they did in the first youthful burst of enthusiasm. In between, the practice of gardening will have made subtle changes to the gardener. In managing an allotment you become tolerant, patient and forward-looking.

There have been occasions, fortunately very few, when vandals at Cowpasture have demonstrated that our tolerance is not limitless. These young thugs might have run the risk of being lynched if they had been caught red-handed one particular summer's night. Instead, they were seen running away by a plotholder who was far too old to give chase. In the morning it was found that ten of the plots had damage of one sort or another. On one a row of runner beans in full flower had been ripped from the ground, while next door the entire onion crop had been pulled up. Lettuces had been kicked about like footballs, marrows had been hurled against huts, and row after row of crops had been trampled and crushed; like all vandalism it was senseless, wanton destruction, impossible for the victim to understand.

The gardens along the seafront at Felixstowe are a prime target for vandals. In spring the beds of massed flowering bulbs are a breathtaking sight. One morning we found hundreds of blooms had been snapped off and the paths were littered with crushed hyacinths, daffodils and tulips. The sense of shock was similar, I imagine, to coming home to find one's house has been burgled.

So the gardener's tolerance and patience do not extend to thieves, vagabonds and vandals. Children who become vandals or thieves or both are the product of homes where respect for one another, for other living things and for other people's property has been eroded; they are the pupils of schools where political considerations and 'progressive' systems have been allowed to obscure the importance of the teaching itself. However, I am reasonably confident that the permissive society has reached its zenith and that we are now seeing a return to self-discipline.

The allotment holder with young children will have them with him at the plot as often as possible so that they can learn alongside their parent the joys of working the land to provide food to take home in triumph. Our four children have each shared in the work and the pleasures of raising crops and I quickly learned a few basic rules about having the family on the plot:

*Make sure the children do not wander to the annoyance of other plotholders.

*Take a good supply of soft drinks and make sure of shade when the going gets a bit too warm.

*Keep a first-aid kit in the hut to cope with minor cuts and stings.

*In your hut, keep any bottles of insecticide and other chemicals out of reach along with knives, secateurs or other potentially damaging tools.

*Try to find something constructive for the children to do, perhaps tending a part of the plot themselves where they can grow a few crops of their own choosing and some flowers for cutting.

*Encourage them to find out about the other inhabitants of the plot – the wild flowers, insects, and the visiting birds and animals.

If your town or district has an allotment holders' association, then join it because it gives you that bit of public muscle in brushes with bureaucracy. If the pressures build up, extra help and advice can be obtained from the National Allotments Society.

The local association will often encourage family participation in the plots by providing a play area for children when they tire of helping. Membership also enables one to buy seed potatoes, lime and fertilisers and peat in bulk at trade prices. If a bulk order is given by the association to the seedsman, very attractive discounts – as much as 25 per cent – are given, and local stockists and garden centres will usually give members a discount on tools.

In Staffordshire I was the founder secretary of the Rickerscote and District Allotment Holders' Association back in 1956. The comradeship of working on our plots with our families was reinforced by evening meetings in the winter for talks by experts, visits to places of interest to the gardener, and our own flower and vegetable shows. Here, in Felixstowe, we belong to the Port of Felixstowe Horticultural Society which covers the interests of private gardener and allotment holder alike.

3

A NEW WORLD
TO EXPLORE

The target is to get the digging done by Christmas, and I have now had plenty of experience of what this involves.

It takes seven minutes to dig a row 15ft wide and 6in deep. Allowing for pauses to admire the scenery, ease the back or to chat up the attendant robin and blackbirds, one can dig eight rows in an hour. That's an area of about 60sq ft. So to dig a 10-rod plot from end to end requires an outlay of about forty hours, bearing in mind that a part will be carrying winter crops and will not require attention until late spring. Starting anew on land heavily infested with perennial weeds such as couch grass, thistle and bindweed would require from two to three times the man-hours.

Some of the younger tenants at Cowpasture prefer to let their plots lie fallow during the winter and then rotovate them in early spring, turning in the weeds along with top-dressed manure and compost. Rotovating is a great time-saver. A 10-rod plot can be cultivated quite comfortably in a morning provided the top growth is not too dense and the manure is thoroughly rotted. If the winter has been mild enough to give a jungle of weeds, it is easier to hand-scythe the weeds to ground level and stack them on the compost heap. Then the manure is spread and rotovating can begin with the aim of giving the top 6in of soil a complete churning. What this does to the friendly earthworm population I shudder to think.

21

Regular, indeed annual, mucking accounts for the high fertility of Cowpasture plots. My favourite country writer, Adrian Bell, says in *Men and Fields* that a Suffolk farmworker told him:

> 'If people ate more of what's grown with muck, there'd not be half the illness about. People say what's grown with artificial manure does you as much good as what's grown with muck. But I know that's wrong.
>   What's grown with chemicals may look all right, but it ain't got the stay in it.'

And that's my philosophy too.

Cowpasture has a light to medium loam of about 14 to 18in over a deep layer of crag, a type of shelly sand that underlies most of the eastern parts of Suffolk and Norfolk. The topsoil quickly dries out so a plentiful supply of humus is essential. This word humus is often misapplied, so it might be worth quoting an international expert on the subject. E. B. Balfour in *The Living Soil* says, 'Humus gives to soil its texture, its stability and much of its capacity for retaining moisture. Humus is a product of decomposition of plant and animal residues through the agency of micro-organisms.'

But even with adequate humus, Cowpasture is one of the most difficult parts for a vegetable gardener to cope with. Felixstowe has the lowest average annual rainfall at 20.9in of anywhere in the United Kingdom, and is second in the national league for sunshine hours, making it a wonderful place for the holidaymaker. It has, too, winds that come unchecked from the Arctic, and briny winds that howl off the North Sea, bringing down bean poles in the autumn, and fences and roof tiles in the winter.

We know that each year will bring a period of drought, usually a three- to four-week spell without a drop of rain. If this happens in April and May and coincides with a prolonged bout of easterly or north-easterly winds, then we really are in trouble: in these conditions seedlings, struggling to survive the drought, can be scorched by the wind and will die unless given some help.

Looking at the records for the past ten years I see that in six of them April and May have brought long spells of dry anticyclonic weather with well below average rainfall and north-easterly winds. In February or March, with the rain curtaining down on to already sodden soil, it is difficult to visualise the land six or eight weeks ahead – dried out a spit deep. But that is becoming the norm.

Another aspect of rotovating an already cultivated plot is the necessity to plan the cropping to accommodate the machine. This can be tricky because the priority in planning should always go to the rotation of brassicas to forestall clubroot.

Clubroot is the deadliest disease of brassicas, hitting farmer and amateur grower alike, and there is no cure. It is a fungus which is present in the soil almost everywhere in the world. It remains dormant, sleeping in the soil, and can only be kept that way by denying it the host of any member of the cabbage family in successive years. Brussels sprouts, cabbages, cauliflowers, kale, kohlrabi, turnips, swedes and radishes are all liable to attack, and so are wallflowers and the weeds charlock and shepherd's purse. The effects are revolting: the plant wilts and becomes stunted and, when dug up, the roots are found to have knobs or swellings. When these are cut open you have a slimy, stinking mess.

So the remedy is to starve the dormant fungus spores by ensuring that brassicas are not grown on the same patch of land more than once in three years. This is an effective control where clubroot is not virulent. As an extra precaution it is wise to use liberal amounts of lime on the brassica patch – up to 2lb a square yard of hydrated lime forked into the top spit is the recommended dose. I also sprinkle calomel dust into the planting holes of the young cauliflower plants because these seem particularly prone to attack by clubroot. Good housekeeping, by hoeing weeds off the plot, is also vital in areas where clubroot has got a grip.

Rotation of the brassicas will not solve the problem of that other major enemy of the cabbage tribe, the cabbage root fly. Fortunately, there are proprietary chemicals to control this pest, though I prefer the old technique of using tarred felt discs.

The cabbage root fly lays its eggs on the surface alongside the stems of the brassicas. Between May and August these hatch and become maggots which burrow into the stem causing severe damage and, eventually, the death of the plant. The discs of roofing felt, which you make about 4in in diameter with a hole at the centre and a slit to allow the disc to be slipped over the young plant, are put in position at planting-out time. They not only deter the cabbage root fly, but also serve as a mulch, retaining moisture to give the root system a flying start.

Fortunately, our predecessors on the plots were meticulous in practising rotation, so at Cowpasture we have little trouble from clubroot. But, of course, that could change rapidly.

The 10-rod plots are mostly 15ft wide by 150ft long, while the 20-rod plots are 300ft long. Because these dimensions give a long and narrow oblong, rotovating has to be done from end to end, while digging is done from side to side. I reckon that for a family of four the winter crops of sprouts, cabbages, savoys, cauliflowers and sprouting broccoli, with spring greens following on, are going to occupy at least a quarter of a 10-rod plot from June through to the following April. If you are also partial to leeks and want a couple of rows of swedes, then a third of the plot will always be carrying crops that need rotating and every third year it will be bang in the middle.

On the whole I feel mechanical cultivation of a vegetable plot does not give the land the attention it deserves. I want to build up the humus content of my plot so that in the dry spells my crops get maximum help from the moisture held in the soil. They will not, most times, come through smiling, but they survive. At the same time, I want to give maximum encouragement to the earthworms. I know my soil is in good heart if, as I dig, I turn up one or more fat pink earthworms in each spadeful.

24

The American author Aldo Leopold defines soil fertility as 'the capacity of soil to receive, store and transmit energy'. So as well as fighting drought I am also aiming to give my plot compost, manure and my two-handed energy so that I, not a machine, become a vital link in an ecological chain. This was superbly summed up by Professor R. Lindsay Rodd in a lecture in Senate House, London University, in 1957. He said:

> Since human health and soil fertility can both be expressed as their capacity to absorb, store and release energy over a continuing period, it seems highly probable that the same foods may vary in health value in accordance with the level of fertility of the soils in which they were grown.
>
> We measure food production in terms of yield, or quantity per unit area, but the real measure is not mere quantity but total human health value of the crop produced.
>
> From this it follows naturally that there is a new world to explore in agro-medical-ecological research, because in the final analysis, the function of land is to maintain human health, and from the handful of soil on the one hand to the loaf of bread on the other this should never be lost sight of in what goes on between.

We are extremely fortunate in having plentiful supplies of seaweed. After the first gales of October or November the beach has a line of bladder-wrack and driftweed which can be spread on the land as it is or composted. Seaweed was used in great quantities by nurserymen on the south coast in Victorian times and was also composted with surplus sprats and herrings.

It provides humus and boron, bromide, calcium, copper, iodine, iron, magnesium, phosphorous, potassium and sodium; it has the same nitrogen content as stable manure, double the potash, and slightly more organic matter. Additionally, it has a high content of salt. I find it particularly valuable for asparagus and beetroots, both marine species, and all brassicas. But it is too good to reserve for particular crops, so I ensure that one-third of my plot gets a dressing of seaweed every year. The other two-thirds will get compost or pig manure.

All vegetables need nitrogen, potash and phosphates at all

stages of their growth. They also need traces of boron, magnesium, iron, copper, and so on. Organic gardeners usually have no problems about providing the right balance of trace elements because properly made compost does the job the natural way. And there's a bonus if seaweed is also used. But a recurring problem on Cowpasture's lightish land is boron deficiency and it seems aggravated by drought. Over-liming is said to be one cause. Another possibility is that in long dry spells the earthworm population goes deeper into the subsoil – in normal conditions the worms bring the minerals up from the lower levels of the soil to near the surface where they become readily available to the plants.

Boron deficiency causes browning of the curd of cauliflowers, crown canker in beetroot, and brown heart in turnips and swedes. The latter is particularly annoying because it is only discovered when a root is cut open in the kitchen ready for cooking. The brown rings running through the flesh tell the story and it is useless to put the roots into the pot because the texture will be woody and the flavour bitter.

A boron deficiency can be remedied by applying borax, but the amount needed is minute, and too much can do a lot of harm. In the event, it is too late to do any good for the root crops once the deficiency has been discovered, so I hope for a natural balance to be struck by the joint action of compost, seaweed and worms.

Potassium deficiency is to be expected on light soils because potassium is highly soluble and is readily leached from the upper region to the lower levels. It causes scorching of the leaf edges of French and runner beans and patchy ripening of outdoor tomatoes. But the most serious effect is on gooseberry bushes. The symptoms are leaf scorch, poor cropping and premature leaf fall. The treatment is regular mulching with compost, although I find it takes two seasons for the bushes to recover their vigour.

No self-respecting vegetable gardener will be without a compost heap in the making. Some experts advocate the compost-only technique for vegetables. But in my twenty-five years' experience I have never been able to grow enough green-stuff to compost, or collect enough other materials to add to the heap to provide sufficient well-made compost for my needs. Even on a 3-acre smallholding, the supply of home-grown materials had to be augmented with bales of half-rotted straw.

With a 10-rod plot and a keen eye for waste that others do not want – your local supermarket throws away sackloads of tired vegetables and spoiled fruit every week – you should be able to make enough compost to give 5 rods a thorough dressing every year. So one ought to back up the compost with another organic fertiliser. At Cowpasture we are fortunate in having ready access to supplies of spent mushroom compost from the mushroom farm at Trimley, stable manure from local riding stables, and pig manure from farms at Kirton and Martlesham.

For heavy soils, there's nothing to beat well-rotted stable manure. On our lighter soil, pig manure is ideal. It is slow-acting, heavy, and able to retain a lot of moisture in dry spells. From early October onwards scarcely a day goes by without a trailer-load of this evil-smelling pig muck arriving at the plots. One load of approximately 3 tons is sufficient for a 10-rod plot, but it must be allowed to rot or 'make', so the earlier one can get it, the better.

Almost every tenant at Cowpasture has manure delivered year in, year out. Eddie, for example, has farmed 20 rods for forty years and every year has had a 3-ton load from either Bucklesham or Martlesham. Forty years ago a load cost 5s (25p) delivered. Ten years ago it was £4, now it is £8.

An exception to the mucking tradition is Frank, who has had a 10-rod plot for seven years and has never given it manure. Instead he buys bags of spent mushroom compost and sprinkles this into the drills when sowing and into the holes when planting out. He claims the results are as good as those produced with manure, but I am not sure about that. Mushroom compost can contain quite large lumps of lime which break down slowly and, used year after year, build up highly alkaline pockets which many crops find distasteful.

A newcomer who, two years ago, took over a 15-rod plot has used no manure, compost or artificial fertiliser. His crops have done extremely well, but only because there was a bank of nutrients in the soil from the years when the previous tenant kept hens on the plot.

Some Cowpasture gardeners leave their digging until the turn of the year, believing that this prevents winter rain leaching nutrients from the manure and compost, but I think this has snags. Perhaps the major one is that spring digging leaves the soil open and uncompacted so that many crops, particularly sprouts, cauliflowers and onion sets, fail to give a good account of themselves. There is also the chance of a hard winter of deep frost that drags on into March with the ground so frozen that it is impossible to get a spade into it.

Frost is a good friend to the vegetable grower. If the soil is turned by the spade and left in slabs, the frost breaks down the lumps to give, eventually, a readily worked friable finish. It also controls mealy aphids and whitefly which, after mild winters, can build up to massive populations on the winter greens. It has another effect on some crops, subtle but important: it gives celery, parsnips and sprouts extra flavour, a nuttiness that makes a world of difference.

We used to reckon on some pretty hard frosts in November here in Suffolk, but there seems to be a gradual change to later winters that don't begin to bite until mid-January but stay around until late April.

If you can only get on to the plot at the weekends, to get the digging done by Christmas calls for a sustained effort and dry weather. But if you are successful, you can enjoy the year-end holiday all the more for having one less chore to carry into the New Year. As you tuck into the turkey, the soil bacteria on the plot are breaking down the manure and compost into readily assimilated plant foods and humus, and the earthworms are facing a good long spell undisturbed by man or machine.

I used to think that the earthworm hibernated in winter until I realised that the surface dressing of compost, seaweed and manure, waiting to be dug in, was being taken by fractions into the topsoil by the worms. In fact, worms only go deep and pause from their internal ploughing of the soil during drought or hard frost.

Yet another advantage of getting the digging done by Christmas is the comforting knowledge that no time will be lost in making a start with planting the onion sets or early potatoes or whatever it is that starts off your gardening year.

If lime is needed for next year's brassicas, it can be spread in early February with no fear that it will have an adverse effect on the manure turned in a couple of months earlier.

No allotment gardener should rely solely on artificial fertilisers for soil fertility. The only chemical fertiliser I use is Growmore, an all-round balanced mixture of sulphate of ammonia, superphosphate of lime and sulphate of potash. It was developed, I believe, in the 1939-45 War and is a trustworthy, economical booster for some crops. I sprinkle a little when planting out sprout and cauliflower plants and I give the onion and asparagus beds a dressing twice a year; the rule with Growmore is 'little and often' rather than one big dose.

The celery trench and onions also get dressings of weathered soot. The pundits say there is virtually no value in this practice because soot contains only minute amounts of plant food and can contain harmful tars and sulphur. Certainly, the nitrogen content is small, but it is released very slowly and I have found soot beneficial in keeping slugs off the celery and giving a tonic lift to onions in May and sprouts in October. In some parts of the country gardeners still use soot to darken the soil in spring so that it absorbs more of the sun's warmth, but I have not seen this done at Cowpasture.

Taking over a plot requires a once-off and totally different plan. With the tenancy at Cowpasture running from October, the incoming tenant can get most of the plot prepared for spring cropping.

In Staffordshire I was one of the tenants on a new allotment site – a virgin meadow. Then the order of the day was double digging to get the turf face down at the bottom of the trench. We were aware that the topsoil was holding a thriving community of leatherjackets and, possibly, wireworms. Luckily, as we dug we had the company of robins, blackbirds and thrushes who rummaged over every spadeful and decimated the inhabitants.

Unless one knows the recent history of the plot being taken over, caution is advised in the matter of manuring and liming. No harm will come from missing the mucking that first year of tenancy, but every effort should be made to learn what the previous tenant's rotation plan involved. Usually, the neighbouring tenants will have all the answers so that you can continue the cycle without a break.

Wherever I have been in my gardening life, couch grass has been with me, and one can always count on it being present on new or neglected plots. I have found there's only one effective way of dealing with couch grass, thistles, bindweed and nettles, and that's digging them out. Couch grass – or squitch, scutch, twitch or bog grass – used to be boiled and the liquor drunk to alleviate gout and rheumatism, but that's about the only kindly thing I have heard tell about the weed. It does spread rapidly, downwards and outwards, so that one season of neglect can allow a build-up.

Some experts recommend rotovating at least twice within four to six weeks on badly infested land. Rake up the roots brought to the surface, let them dry off, and burn them. But if the land is also thick with thistles, coltsfoot or, God forbid, horsetail and oxalis, then rotovating is not going to help. Chemical control of these weeds is possible but costly, so I have always relied on digging as the main deterrent with regular hoeing during the growing season for my crops.

If the land were entirely clear of perennial weeds, it might be possible to use the no-digging method of cultivation on part of the plot. Dr W. E. Shewell-Cooper is probably the best-known advocate of this technique and anyone who wanted to give it a try could do no better than study the doctor's advice in his book *The Complete Vegetable Grower.*

Briefly, the idea is to cover the surface of the soil in early spring with a layer of at least 1in of compost or sedge peat, having first sprinkled the soil with a balanced organic fertiliser such as fish meal. Seeds are sown before being covered with the peat or compost, but plants are dibbled through the mulch and into the soil.

Fish meal fertiliser is now difficult to come by and very expensive, so no doubt another organic food would be satisfactory. The layer of compost or peat keeps annual weeds in check and, serving as a mulch, gives moisture-retaining help to the plants which is especially welcome in dry seasons.

There is a snag, of course. To cover a 10-rod allotment plot with a 1in layer of compost would require an enormous quantity – far beyond the resources of the average plotholder – while to use sedge peat as an alternative would mean buying ten 1cwt bales for every 100sq yd, or thirty bales a year for the entire plot.

I would dearly like to give the no-digging technique an airing on my plot – or at least on part of it, because I could never make enough compost to mulch the whole plot. But I am afraid I would never be able to say, hand on heart, that the land was thoroughly clear of perennial weeds so that a start could be made.

The definition of a weed is that it is a plant growing where it's not wanted. Weeds are certainly not wanted in the vegetable patch. They compete with the crops for space, soil nutrients, sun and air, so the hoe must be kept active to hold them in check.

The Soil Association publishes a useful booklet exploring the natural fact that a plant flourishes best where soil and environment are favourable to its growth. The types of weed and their placing on the plot can indicate mineral deficiencies, poor drainage, or lack of humus.

The soil lies in wait for man to make a mistake and the

commonest mistake man makes at Cowpasture is failure to check weed growth before seeds form. Chickweed is abundant and, in a mild winter, will quickly carpet soil that has been turned over ready for the spring. Each chickweed plant will produce up to 2,500 seeds and these can survive for up to twenty-five years. Fortunately, these young weed plants are readily dealt with by the hoe or a light forking over in the early spring. Chickweed contains manganese and potassium, so it is an excellent subject for the compost heap.

One winter all digging at the plot was completed by the end of November. On the patch where I had grown onions, keeping it extra clear of weeds, the soil crumbled as I turned it over. In Suffolk mild winters almost always mean above-average rainfall, and this particular year heavy rain in December flattened the soil surface of the old onion bed to give a fine tilth. By Christmas this was covered in seedling weeds, mostly chickweed. In a square foot I counted 108 chickweed seedlings – about 900 to the square yard. So on that 25sq yd part of the plot the chickweed population was possibly 22,500 plants or rather more than the human population of Felixstowe.

Another annual weed, groundsel, is present all the year on the Cowpasture plots. Because its seeds are wind-borne by fluffy parachutes we are unlikely to do more than keep groundsel at manageable proportions; it will flower even in the depth of winter. Each mature plant produces up to 1,000 seeds which have little or no dormancy and can germinate quickly so that in a single year there may be two or three generations of seed-bearing plants. Birds are fond of groundsel seeds, some of which will be scattered far and wide in their droppings.

Other common annual weeds at Cowpasture include goosefoot or all-seed which is a prolific weed on Suffolk's light soils, meadow grass, sun spurge, charlock, fat hen, poppy and shepherd's purse. The latter flowers and seeds throughout the year, but mainly in spring and summer. As with chickweed, the seeds of shepherd's purse can be buried for up to thirty years until they eventually reach the surface and start into growth.

And, as with groundsel, two or three generations are possible in a year. Fortunately, shepherd's purse is one of the easiest weeds to pull up by hand and, being rich in calcium, is a good subject for composting.

One of the weeds I look forward to seeing each year is scented mayweed or wild chamomile. This is a lime-loving plant that appears in great numbers after a piece of the plot has had a winter dressing of hydrated lime. The mature plants have daisy-like flowers, and when the plants are crushed underfoot or pulled by hand the heady perfume is a smell of summer as characteristic as strawberries and cream.

In years of drought the field bindweed prospers on my plot. It has very attractive bell-shaped pink and white flowers, but otherwise has most unpleasant habits, using any other plant as a host to climb and dominate. Worse still is what is happening underground. The tap root of bindweed, white and sinuous, goes down and down in search of moisture, and while other more shallow-rooting plants are suffering in the drought, bindweed bounds ahead.

Coltsfoot and dandelion seem to favour heavy soils and don't give us much trouble at Cowpasture, but horsetail rampages through our light land and over the years has become a major menace. This flowerless perennial is the oldest species of plant still surviving, with an ancestry that goes back millions of years. It has rhizomatous wire-like roots that break easily, so that hoeing and digging distribute pieces that rapidly become new plants. The rhizomes go very deep: when my neighbour was digging a well on his plot he found a root that went down 5ft and then branched off horizontally.

Tom, who has had to cope with horsetail for all of sixty years, says that there is no way to rid the plot of this weed, but it can be controlled by digging, hoeing and burning. I checked with Fisons, who confirmed that this weed is the bugbear of farmers and gardeners alike, but that eradication is possible by using one of the growth-regulator herbicides such as MCPA, MCPB or 2, 4-D. On the brighter side, the Soil Association says that because horsetail is rich in silica it can be put to work to help the gardener. An infusion made from this weed can be used to beat black spot on roses and mildew on soft fruit and vegetables. It can also be used to prevent mint rust, says the Association. The recipe is to put two good handfuls of fresh horsetail shoots in a pan and cover with water; bring to the boil and simmer for 20 minutes. Cover and leave overnight. Then strain the liquor and dilute with two parts of water. You now have a liquid that can be sprayed on to the leaves of affected plants.

The old name for horsetail is pewterwort and it was once widely used to clean pewter ware. The stems and leaves carry deposits of tiny crystals of silica which act like fine sandpaper or wire wool when cleaning the metal.

On the advice of the Soil Association I have tried the technique of symbiosis, or encouraging plants to be friends, but without any marked success. Mr F. C. King, gardener-in-chief at Levens Hall in Cumbria and an expert on composting, reckoned that the onion crop was improved by allowing weeds to grow unchecked in the onion patch after the first week of July. The theory here is that the weeds rob the onions of nitrogen and so improve their keeping quality. I haven't tried this because I have never had any difficulty in keeping onions even for as long as ten months.

The symbiotic relationship of aromatic herbs with almost all vegetable crops has been written about many times. Herbs such as rosemary and thyme are said to have an invigorating effect on their vegetable neighbours and, at the same time, repel destructive insects. So a few years ago I planted six well-rooted cuttings of rosemary and another six cuttings of lavender. The rosemary I sited at various points on the edges of the plot, while the lavender became a southern-end border. But the results were inconclusive. Adjacent crops were no better than I had come to expect and there was no marked difference in the population of insect pests.

In five years rosemary cuttings become fair-sized bushes that occupy a lot of space. A sprig of rosemary certainly does something for roast lamb, but my bushes would have garnished every Sunday joint in East Anglia and still flourished. In preference to mass extermination I decided to keep two rosemary bushes and give the other four a new lease of life elsewhere. So now the hedge on the south-western perimeter of Cowpasture is the new home for the rosemary plants and they are revelling in it. The lavender remains as a border on the plot and the dried flower spikes scent the linen drawers at home.

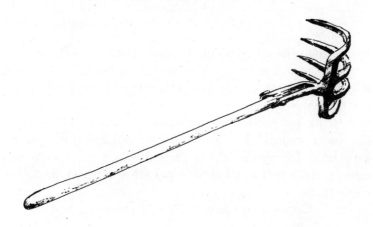

4

NOT JUST
A CABBAGE PATCH

By the time the oil runs out we shall have had to relearn the methods of our forefathers. Already there are signs that farming is looking back over its shoulder at the days before it underwent the mechanical revolution. If you tend the soil it is always interesting and sometimes profitable to listen to the advice of the older hands. I enjoy reading William Cobbett on gardening. He speaks about the cultivation of vegetables a century and a half ago, but his ideas are as fresh as the day he wrote them.

This is Cobbett on the technique of growing peas:

> A sufficient distance [between rows] is one of the greatest things in the raising of peas, whether they be sticked or whether they be not; and they never ought to be sowed too thickly in the row.
> I never tried it, but I verily believe that a row of peas, each plant being at two or three inches distance from the other, would bear a greater crop than in the usual way.

I tried it with a row of Gloriosa, a new introduction sent to me for trial but in such sort supply that there were insufficient seeds for a full row had they been sown thickly in a 6in wide drill. Sown in a 1in deep drill, with the seeds 3in apart, the plants grew extremely vigorously and produced a wonderful show of flowers. Unfortunately, it was a summer of severe drought, so the yield was affected.

E. R. Janes in his excellent book *The Vegetable Garden* tells this story:

> A seed merchant contracted with a farmer to grow several acres of a new variety of peas for seed. After sowing rain fell incessantly for many weeks and germination was bad. So bad was it that in places the seedlings were a yard or more apart.
>
> The farmer, greatly perturbed, sent for the seed merchant to inspect the seedlings as he wished to plough in the crop and grow something else.
>
> It was a valuable new variety, of which little more seed existed, so the seed merchant persuaded the farmer to carry on, promising to compensate should the crop be poor.
>
> The soil was good, well cultivated, the summer was favourable, and the farmer kept the crop clean. The seedlings, having room to develop, grew into bushy specimens self-supporting by their own lateral shoots and, although so far apart, finally covered the ground.
>
> It was a magnificent sight and the crop, although splendid from a consumer's point of view, was difficult for the farmer to handle, for the many-branched plants provided pods for a long period – exactly what is needed in a garden for household use.

Another year I tried Hurst Green Shaft in a single row 6in apart. I covered them with cloches and, when the seedlings were about 4in tall and looking the picture of health, took the cloches away and gave each plant a bushy stick for support. The following morning I arrived at my plot to see a family of partridges skeetering down the path, having feasted off my young pea plants.

Without the oil-based fertilisers and the internal combustion engine, the day of the mixed farm will return, presumably, and the horseman will again become skilled in the mysteries and magic of the craft. I have a hand-written notebook in which a Suffolk horseman more than a hundred years ago listed in beautiful copperplate some eighty-five recipes for success with horses. Some are secret potions, handed on by 'The Whisperers' or the Society of Horsemen from that distant past when the farm revolved around the horse and the head horseman was a king among men.

Here. is the recipe for a spring tonic for the horses:

Celandine, parsley, breakstone, rue, mallows, sheep's parsley. Cut it in with the chaff and corn and it will keep them from lingering.

And another for 'alluring rats':

Twenty drops of anniseed, 10 drops of rhondium, 40 drops of oil of ambergris, 50 drops of musk, one root of valerian bruised, 20 drops of oil of rats. Put them all into a bottle. When you lay the mixture or set your traps dress your hands with the same oils and you may do as you please with them after the stupefaction. Lay that for one night. The second night 1oz of nux vomica, $\frac{1}{2}$ oz of dulwes indicus. Braid and bruise them, add two table spoonfuls of liquid of laudium, mix them with clean wheatflour and some sugar, about two ounces. Boiled up the fourth night to kill them, add to the above 3 table spoonfuls of prepared arsenic.

If you are wondering how to get hold of oil of rats, this is what you must do:

Take the bodies of the female rats, as many as you think proper. With the fat of the inside, loins and kidney, take the liver of the same, put them into a jar. Tie them down close and sit it in an oven after the bread is drawn. When the oil is extracted put it into a bottle.

Meanwhile, President Carter warns the American people to reduce their consumption of energy or face catastrophe. 'With the exception of preventing war, this is the greatest challenge our country will face in our lifetime,' he said. The United States is the most wasteful country, each American using the equivalent of 60 barrels (2,100 gallons) of oil each year.

Dr Stuart Hill, of McGill University in Quebec, a professor of zoology, told a farming conference in Maine that the West had to look for a post-industrial agriculture system. We have to find a way of supplying our food needs on an individual basis or on an individual family basis.

Conventional agriculture has gone wrong, the professor said, because it is no longer directed at trying to create human health. It is directed towards productivity and profit, which compromises the objective of nutritional quality and health. It is addicted to high-energy fossil fuel and high input levels of resources which are to a large degree finite and cannot be relied upon for ever. And, thirdly, conventional farming since 1940 has been damaging to the environment to an extent that in some parts of the United States and Britain is not far short of catastrophic.

It will take many years for the damage to be made good once a start is made but, as has been demonstrated time without number, no government is going to risk votes to set the ball in motion. We ought, for example, to be planning for the family-sized farm using horse power. It will take at least twenty years to breed as many horses as were being used in 1939, and we should probably need twice the number, yet a start has not been made.

Similarly, we should be turning towards an ecological system of plant breeding. 'We should select plants', says Dr Hill, 'that meet the needs of the local population and that stress nutritional quality, tastiness, perhaps resistance to pests and diseases, ability to compete with weeds, suitability to local conditions, ability to improve soils and low energy dependency.'

On the same theme as Dr Hill Sir Emrys Jones, Principal of the Royal Agricultural College, said:

> The time has come for young men in farming to rethink agricultural systems evolved over the last 30 years. Students now being trained should realise that they could be farming without fuel oil by their 50th birthday.
>
> They will also be without inorganic fertilisers and most of the insecticides and pesticides we now take for granted unless the scientists come to the rescue. If I were a young man, I would certainly not bank on their coming up with the answer.

Those of us who farm our allotments or otherwise grow our own fruit and vegetables are not dismayed at the prospect. In ourselves we have the most efficient machine ever devised, the most economical source of energy and one with an inbuilt system for recycling waste. We already select plants for quality, flavour, suitability for local conditions and the ability to satisfy our families.

I have a twinge of conscience about two crops I grow on my plot at Cowpasture: asparagus and strawberries. They are the epitome of luxury when measured against the basic needs of all those thousands on the waiting lists for allotments. But God forbid that our plots should become just cabbage patches.

Asparagus grew wild in Britain in 2,000 BC when the Windmill Hill people settled on the Downs of southern England and began tilling the soil with their stone tools. At what stage it became a cultivated plant we cannot be sure, but the Romans, those superb gardeners who brought to England all the basic hand tools – hoe, rake, spade and axe – and the sophistication of heated greenhouses, developed the growing of asparagus to a peak. I have not been able to discover any reference to the Roman equivalent of our modern varieties of asparagus, but according to the King of Asparagus, Mr A. W. Kidner, the variety is unimportant anyway.

The fifty 3-year-old crowns that were to start my asparagus bed were Connover's Colossal. They were a fiftieth birthday present from my wife, Margaret, and the order was placed with a famous Wisbech grower for delivery on or near the anniversary day, 29 April. But weather conditions delayed lifting and the crowns arrived on 9 May.

I had prepared a 6ft wide bed across the full 15ft of the plot. The weather was perfect for setting out the crowns: a half-inch of rain the previous day, then a week of cloudy but warm days. Deep digging had been essential to rid the site of perennial weeds. The finished bed was about 6in proud of the rest of the plot, having been capped with a dressing of composted seaweed and 2 or 3in of well-rotted pig manure.

That first year it was a great disappointment to find that, of the fifty crowns so carefully planted, only twenty or so were alive, but the experts said that a 50 to 60 per cent loss in transplanting is quite usual. Another annoyance was the resulting gaps in the bed, with some fairly large areas where, perhaps, up to six crowns had failed. Subsequently, I was able to plug the gaps by transplanting. The first and second years we took only token bunches from the bed, but later we had a good succession of the most succulent sticks imaginable.

I made a mistake, when planting the bed, in making it 6ft wide; it is far better to have two beds, each 3ft wide, with an alleyway between, then you don't have to walk over the beds to cut the crop.

Cutting is a fairly tricky operation. One needs a very sharp, thin-bladed knife to cut through each shoot about 4in below the surface, and this has to be done without damaging other shoots yet to emerge.

I give the bed a winter dressing of compost and seaweed and, apart from cutting down the asparagus fern in the autumn and keeping weeds at bay, there is no other work involved. With luck, we shall still be cutting bundles from that bed in fifteen years' time – more than we shall be able to eat. So I am looking forward to being able to give friends a springtime taste that defies description.

When planning the plot, experience has taught me that it is vitally important to give a lot of thought to the siting of currants, berries and your asparagus bed. Three years ago I planted a Himalayan Giant blackberry cane. I put it midway across the plot and then strained two wires from stakes at either side. The intention was to train the canes each way, cordon fashion. Not for nothing is it called giant. It grew and grew, east, west, north and south. The harder I pruned, the more vigorous it became. We are not jam eaters and there's a limit to our capacity for making blackberry wine, so in autumn I cut the monster back, dug it out and gave it to a friend who is giving it more room than I can spare.

Unless space is severely restricted, a place for strawberries should be high on the list, although Lawrence Hills recommends a four-year rotation for strawberries – and onions – as a means of avoiding pests and diseases. William Butler in the seventeenth century said of the strawberry, 'Doubtless God could have made a better berry, but doubtless God never did.'

Here in eastern England we know a thing or two about strawberry growing. In the Wisbech area of the Fens there are some very big growers with 300 acres of strawberries giving an income, at 1977 prices, of £70,000 a year. And in north-east Essex contract growers supply hundreds of tons of fruit for the commercial jam producers. If the aim is self-sufficiency, then three 15ft rows of strawberry plants will provide enough fruit in their second and third years to satisfy the needs of a family of four.

In Cobbett's time the market gardener practised forcing on a scale unheard-of today because, of course, we can open a tin or go to the freezer for our out-of-season foods. In *The English Gardener* he gives a month-by-month calendar of jobs to be done, and for January he recommends forcing asparagus, potatoes, French beans, rhubarb, seakale, and strawberries in pots.

The oldest variety of strawberry still being grown is Royal Sovereign and it is still unbeaten for flavour and good looks. It was raised by that prolific plant breeder, Thomas Laxton, at Bedford in about 1890 and was the offspring of the marriage of Noble with King of the Earlies.

Royal Sovereign is an early variety that could be severely hurt by Cowpasture's exposure to May frosts and searing easterly winds. So I chose the mid-season variety Cambridge Favourite and sacrificed earlier picking for its good resistance to botrytis, frost and mildew and its love of the light loam. Cambridge Favourite, together with many other varieties with the prefix, was developed by Mr D. Boyes, director of the Horticultural Research Station at Cambridge. After the 1939-45 War, Mr Howard Jones of Kingsley, Hampshire, took over the trials of some 680 of the Cambridge varieties. The result is a selection of superb varieties that can truly be said to have reached a peak of refinement for flavour, disease-resistance, shape, colour and yield.

I have grown strawberries for many years and have almost always used straw between the plants to protect them from splashing. One year I used black polythene sheets, but that was a disaster. The idea was to protect the fruits and hasten ripening, but that year we had an exceptionally dry May and June and scorching sunshine. So, many of the plants dried out and shrivelled before the berries were able to swell.

Straw has several disadvantages. It delays ripening because it reflects the sunlight; it actually encourages weeds; and it invariably hides the biggest berries. But it is still inexpensive, and if there are only a couple of rows to consider, most garden shops will sell a sack of loose straw or split a bale. And when it has done its job on the strawberry patch, the straw can be composted.

I intend to use peat from now on. This will come from the boxes of carrots and beetroots that have been in store over the winter. I estimate that a 40kg bag will give a thick enough mulch between and around the plants to protect the berries and suppress the weeds. It will gradually be absorbed into the topsoil to add to the humus that strawberries must have to do well.

Birds are as fond of strawberries as we are, and blackbirds, particularly, make a beeline for the berries the moment they start blushing. The remedy is to cover the rows with netting – the fine-gauge plastic netting such as Netlon is ideal. To aid picking I drive in 3ft stakes 4ft apart each way and then put an old tennis ball on top of each stake by cutting a slit in the ball. The net slides easily over the balls and the whole contraption can be used year after year.

A few of my companions at Cowpasture have more elaborate structures, professionally made cages that cover the strawberries and the raspberry canes, enabling one to move about inside. But, as with the Netlon, it is important to ensure that the sides are well secured. Trying to free a blackbird or thrush that has got under the netting, been unable to find an exit and ended up in a miserable tangle, is no fun for anyone. On one occasion a hedgehog got himself helplessly entangled and must have spent a night of acute discomfort. Fortunately, when I was able to cut him free, he scampered off along the path apparently none the worse.

5

WELCOME TO NEWCOMERS

Taking prizes at a produce show is a very satisfying way of spending an afternoon. It is always reassuring to have one's assessment of a well-grown crop confirmed in competition with others. The Royal Horticultural Society produces a bible for those who organise, exhibit or judge horticultural shows. Called *The Horticultural Show Handbook,* it sets out standards for flowers, fruits and vegetables so that there is consistency and continuity in preparing for and exhibiting in shows wherever in Britain they are held.

There are three criteria used in assessing the merits of vegetables in a show: condition, size and uniformity. Condition involves 'cleanliness, freshness, tenderness and presence or absence of coarseness and blemishes'. Size is 'meritorious if accompanied by quality (but only in those circumstances) as the production of large specimens of good quality requires more skill than the production of small specimens. The size of vegetables most suitable for table use varies with the consumer'. Uniformity is called for in 'size, form and colour'.

Missing from these criteria is another essential feature – flavour. But, of course, it is impossible to judge the flavour of, say, a Primo cabbage or a Detroit beetroot by looking at it on the show bench. The variety, or cultivar as the RHS prefers it to be called, gives a clue as to how those handsome exhibits will perform at the dinner table. Superior flavour is what almost always distinguishes the amateur vegetable grower's produce from the commercially grown equivalent, and superior flavour is the bonus that comes from organic cultivation.

Our home does not have a deep-freeze cabinet because we have convinced ourselves that flavour goes out of the window when food goes into the freezer. E. B. Balfour in *The Living Soil* says there appears to be some, as yet undefined, harm done to foods by long storage of any kind, whether they are frozen, heated and tinned, or dried, though probably drying is the least harmful process. That damage might be the reason why frozen foods lack the flavour of fresh.

In vegetables I prefer compactness to rotundness. Green vegetables are best if taken to the table within an hour or so of harvesting. If the meal is for two people only, then your average cabbage or cauliflower is too big for one meal and the remnants too stale to use later.

Thompson and Morgan, the Ipswich seedsmen, have introduced me to several interesting new varieties, some of which have survived being given a fanfare announcement as novelties to become established items in the catalogue. And I give a special welcome to newcomers classified as 'compact'. One of these is Celtic, a winter cabbage that stands well into the New Year. It is a small ballhead coming to the kitchen at 1½ to 2lb when fully mature and, whether cooked or shredded raw for salad use, has an exceptionally fine flavour.

Fanny Craddock has a recipe for this cabbage which brings out the flavour to the full. Slice as thinly as possible into strips like spaghetti. Put into a saucepan with 1in of cold water, a grated small onion and a rounded teaspoonful of salt for each pound of cabbage. Clap on the lid, bring to a fast boil, turn over once, replace the lid and simmer for 7 minutes only. Drain, stir in a walnut-sized piece of butter and a dessertspoonful of fresh chopped parsley.

Unwins, the Cambridgeshire family firm, have two excellent small cabbages in their list. Minicole is an F1 hybrid, interestingly named because colewort was the medieval name for cabbage. It is a round to oval head and stands well without splitting. The other little beauty is Vienna Baby Head which matures after Primo. This, too, keeps in good condition for a long period and resists splitting.

With cabbages and Brussels sprouts it is worth paying the premium for F1 hybrid seeds. These are the offspring of the marriage of two true parent strains and they are more expensive because they are produced under strictly controlled conditions that sometimes involve hand pollination. You pay up to twice as much, but you get a higher rate of germination, increased vigour, and uniformity in size, shape and colour.

The fashion today is for courgettes rather than marrows, and the giant fruits are only in favour for harvest festivals and the produce shows. So at Cowpasture we grow varieties such as Suttons' Tender and True, and Table Dainty, and eat the fruits when they are 4 to 6in long and can be steamed and eaten in their skins. For those who still like a meal of stuffed marrow, Suttons have Green Bush Smallpak, a smaller version of Green Bush Improved, retaining that characteristic delicate flavour.

I grow only the cos type of lettuce which was very popular in Cobbett's time, then declined and only in the seventies has come back into favour. Now we have several self-folding sorts. But the one I like best is a miniature cos – Little Gem – which grows only 6in or so tall, hearts up very rapidly and can be sown for succession from March to August. It is ideal for two people, with little waste and a fine, nutty flavour.

Brussels sprouts can be had in varieties that crop from September until March although, like celery and parsnips, this vegetable is best eaten after a frost has brought on the flavour. Children often develop a strong hatred of this and other 'greens' and over-cooking to a slodgy mess is sometimes to blame. So it is always worth introducing them to raw, shredded sprouts and cabbage – in very small amounts – so they can enjoy the flavour to the full and benefit from the high vitamin C content. We have found that pressure-cooking is the only way to do full justice to all green vegetables, including delicate subjects such as asparagus and courgettes.

With sprouts the F1 hybrids such as Peer Gynt, Achilles, Citadel and Focus in favourable seasons yield nearly half as much again as the older varieties. I like small buttons such as those on Roodnerf Early Button and Peer Gynt F1, and leave the big buttons of Fillbasket to the commercial growers in Bedfordshire. Peer Gynt is a dwarf-growing variety, seldom more than 18in tall, which matures in late October. But a word of warning. I grew a few rows and failed to guard them. Just when they were at their peak I went to Cowpasture one morning to find rabbits had stripped almost every button from the stocky stems of Peer Gynt, while the taller sorts were untouched.

Rabbits, rats, wood pigeons, pheasants and partridges – we get them all at Cowpasture, and a few summers back a coypu was found on the plots. Rows of seedlings can be protected from birds by using black cotton. Make three hoops from 18in lengths of heavy-gauge wire and put one hoop at each end of the row, the third in the middle. Now run the black cotton or nylon thread from hoop to hoop, tying it tightly at each end. Five or six strands will do the trick.

Mice are a menace, taking the pea seeds soon after sowing. Soaking the seed for an hour or so in paraffin is a deterrent and, after sowing, a light dusting of hydrated lime on the surface of the soil gives a bit more protection. Where wood mice are very active the only sure safeguards against their taking the pea seeds are either sowing after the middle of April or covering the rows with cloches. Apart from their raids on the peas, wood mice do not appear to take any other of my crops, so I never persecute them.

If the rows are not cloche-covered, pea guards are essential protection for the young plants against game birds at Cowpasture. One spring I had two rows of Kelvedon Wonder early peas showing about an inch of sturdy growth. I wanted the wire guards for the next two rows, so I transferred them. Overnight, birds – either pheasants or partridges, by the size of their droppings – had pulled up every pea plant and eaten the seed only, leaving the green shoot. So now I keep the guards in place until I am ready to put the pea sticks into the rows.

The remaining hedgerows round about Cowpasture provide pea sticks. So does the council. In March a gang of workmen pollard the trees that line many of the streets in Felixstowe. They lop the new growth off these poor, stunted things they call trees and are only too glad to get rid of the sticks. One year we even persuaded the foreman to dump a trailer load at Cowpasture. If no pea sticks are available, Netlon plastic netting or wire netting can be used, but make sure the stakes you use for support are driven well home. Summer gales can wreak havoc with rows of fully-grown peas.

Sweet, tender garden peas are such an intrinsic part of early summer delights that I tend to give more attention to the half-dozen rows I grow than to anything else on the plot. Peas need a moist soil packed with humus, and because my plot has a shallow layer of loam over the crag, I've devised a technique to hold moisture longer at a level where the pea plants' questing roots can linger.

I take out a trench a spade's depth and width. Into this goes a layer of shredded newspaper that has been soaked in a tub of rainwater for a couple of days. On to this I put a layer of compost followed by a dusting of fish meal or dried blood. Then I put back 2in of topsoil and sow the pea seeds at 3in intervals in a double row 6in apart. A 2in covering of soil goes on next and is firmed and given a light dusting with hydrated lime. Finally, the row is covered with pea guards or cloches.

Kelvedon Wonder is the supreme early pea without rival for yield, sturdiness and flavour. Growth is bushy to a maximum height of 2ft so only a minimum of support is needed. I aim to get two 15ft rows sown in early March for gathering in mid-June, having been covered with cloches for a month to six weeks. I follow with two rows of Onward in late March, and two rows of Hurst Green Shaft in mid-April. The latter produces nine or ten peas in a narrow 4½in pod on plants about 2ft 6in tall; the flavour is exceptional and yield is high in a normal season, though it falls dramatically in drought or unusually cool conditions.

Garden peas are one of the oldest cultivated crops in Britain. The Romans grew them and so did the Anglo-Saxons, and they were often used as a culinary windbreak in East Anglian vineyards. The Flemish gardeners who settled at Sandy in Bedfordshire, at Norwich and Colchester, and at various places in Kent, introduced new ideas in horticulture to England – especially their methods with peas, French beans, carrots and cabbages. But the big breakthrough in pea growing came in the late 1790s with the introduction of the wrinkled marrowfat by Thomas Knight of Herefordshire.

Round peas are hardier than the wrinkled varieties and in favoured southern areas can be sown in late autumn to overwinter and give a very early crop the following spring. But round peas lack the sweet flavour of the marrowfat sorts which contain far more sugar. So, ever since Thomas Knight's achievement, breeders have been trying to produce wrinkled peas that have both the flavour of the marrowfat and the extra hardiness of the round-seeded sorts such as Meteor, Market Gem and Early Bird.

A very heavy cropper is the new variety Gloriosa. It has a fine, sweet flavour, grows only 20in tall, and has the merit of good resistance to cold spells and drought. Another high-yielding variety is Feltham First, closely followed by Gradus, Little Marvel and Progress No 9.

Onward is a superb variety for all-round performance. It has neat, compact growth, but carries its flowers high up the plant, which helps the bees and other pollinators, and aids picking. It was introduced by that great plant breeder W. J. Unwin at Histon, Cambridgeshire. He also gave us The Amateur outdoor bush tomato and, of course, a wonderful range of his beloved sweet peas. Unwins carry on a great tradition of intense interest in plant breeding and old-world courtesy to their customers, and the firm is still owned and controlled by members of W. J.'s family.

Some Cowpasture colleagues sow peas for a long succession of picking from early June through to mid-September, and in more favourable parts of the south and west, growers sow in November for a picking in mid-May.

The pea succession for top flavour and yield is: Kelvedon Wonder or Early Onward sown as soon as possible in March and, preferably, cloched for picking in early June. Follow with Recette, Gloriosa or Gradus in early April for mid-July maturity. A sowing of Onward, Hurst Green Shaft or Lord Chancellor in late April keeps the cook happy into early August, and a final sowing of Kelvedon Wonder at the end of May gives peas into late August.

A French recipe of 1325 recommended cooking peas in half water, half wine, adding butter when cooked. A later recipe, also from France, involves adding the peas to chopped spring onions, lettuce hearts and butter and cooking for an hour over a low heat. We liked both recipes, the latter one being particularly successful with roast duckling.

If you grow your own, don't be miserly over peas. The yield from a 15ft row is 8 to 10lb, and for early varieties, picked young, allow 1lb of peas in the pod per adult; for maincrop, picked full, allow $\frac{3}{4}$lb per adult.

Incidentally, the empty pods make a good country wine, provided you have not used a poisonous spray. To make a gallon of wine, boil 5lb of pods in a gallon of water for about 30 minutes or until tender. Strain off the liquor, add 3lb of granulated sugar and boil for 30 minutes. Put into a fermenting bucket and add the activated wine yeast (a heaped teaspoonful in warm water, allowed to work for 6 hours). Allow to ferment vigorously for a week, then put into a fermenting jar with airlock to finish off – in about three weeks. Syphon off into bottles and restrain yourself from drinking it. This wine, made in July, is throwing a rather dry, delicate bouquet by Christmas. I'm told it is even better the next Christmas.

Because of the summer gales I no longer grow runner beans upwards, and most of my colleagues have given it up, too. I tried the traditional inverted V row using a combination of bean poles and ex-WD telephone wire. I braced and strained the structure and had a magnificent crop of Scarlet Emperor. On 5 September we had a freak thunderstorm and a wind that gusted to 50mph. Down came the beans.

Next year I tried wigwams of a dozen poles pushed well into the soil and tied tightly together at the top with guy ropes for extra protection. The lot came down, prematurely, in the first week of October with such force that most of the plants on the windward side were ripped from the ground. There's no fun in seeing one of our favourite vegetables in a tangled, unusable mess, so I swore 'never again'.

Runner beans provide about the best return of any vegetable, and I like the succession of peas, followed by French beans, then the runners through from early August until the first frost of November.

My runner beans grown 'on the flat' are sown in rows 2ft apart with the seeds a foot apart in the row. When the plants are growing strongly and have made about 16in, I pinch out the growing points. The plants support each other and form a dense carpet of growth that, in a dry season, prevents too rapid a loss of moisture. To encourage maximum production of flowers, straggling shoots are pinched back, and an occasional spray with rainwater at dusk seems to be much appreciated.

Six rows, when fully productive, will cover an area 15ft square and give enough beans to eat fresh two or three times a week with a surplus to salt down for the winter. Picking is not so easy as for those grown upwards, and some of the beans grow sickle-shaped, but otherwise the crop is remarkably trouble-free. I save my own seed from an original stock of Scarlet Emperor, Crusader and Desiree. This last-named variety was introduced by Thompson and Morgan in, I believe, their 1976 list. It is a very good bean indeed, giving a mass of white flowers followed by fleshy pods with excellent flavour.

French beans haven't the distinctive flavour and texture of the runner, but are preferred by some people because, eaten young, they are entirely stringless. I grow two varieties: the old-established Masterpiece and the much newer Limelight. There's about a fortnight's difference in the time they mature. I pick them when they are about 5in long, and Margaret cooks them whole in the pressure cooker for just 4 minutes.

I sow in late April or early May on a piece of the plot that has been liberally manured the previous year – usually where I had the winter greenstuff. The seeds go in 2in deep and 6in apart, in rows a foot apart. This is rather more crowded than the experts recommend, but on windy sites such as Cowpasture, wider spacing would mean providing sticks for support as the mature plants are rather top-heavy and readily keel over in a storm. Slugs love the young shoots, so I sprinkle soot.

French beans do best in a summer that's warm and wet, and come to think of it, what vegetable doesn't? Five rows are needed for self-sufficiency, but I always have an extra row to mature and gather as seed for the following year.

6

WATER – A SCARCE COMMODITY

There is an annual battle against drought at Cowpasture. No year passes without a long spell of very dry weather and since 1970 there has been a succession of summer droughts culminating in the spring and summer record drought in 1976. Few gardeners can have dreamed of the nightmare effects of that drought, and its effects on mature trees are still being felt.

Suffolk has a vast number of elms so our landscape is becoming ravaged as Dutch elm disease picks off these beautiful trees one by one. When we had Cherry Place, our smallholding in west Suffolk, we had to have a 50ft elm felled because of the disease. It is a heartrending sight to watch the majestic growth of a lifetime reduced to logs in an afternoon.

Dutch elm disease first appeared in Britain in 1927. It is spread by a beetle only $\frac{1}{4}$in long. This lays eggs in the bark of the tree and the larvae eat the wood. When they become adult the beetles emerge from the bark and fly off, carrying a fungus with them to infect another host tree. This fungus is the thing that does the damage by blocking the sap channels in the trees so that they rot at the hearts.

Some foresters believe that most mature elms can survive attacks of the disease, and reckon that a winter of very hard frosts will do more good, by destroying the beetles, than felling or lopping. Unfortunately, with the disease at epidemic proportions in southern and eastern England came the driest spring and summer since 1727, and even the strongest elms succumbed.

In the European Community each person uses about 100 gallons of fresh water a day and most of it is flushed down the lavatory. By the year 2000 demand for water is likely to be double what it was in 1970, and supply, unless it is rationed, will fall short of demand. It takes 44,000 gallons of water to make a ton of steel, and 100,000 gallons to make a family car, but only 1 gallon to make a cabbage, so well before 1999 we shall have to decide on our priorities.

Cowpasture has no piped water and only three wells. Two were dug in 1935, and the third – my neighbour's – in 1975. Each is about 18ft deep, going through a 15ft layer of crag, and each has about 3 to 4ft of water. But almost every plot has a hut and every hut a rain butt or tank. So our first line of defence in the battle against drought is 50 to 100 gallons of rainwater collected over the year, and as it also has to be used for puddling in the brassica plants and leeks, this source of water quickly dries up. Then there's the tedious task of filling containers at home to take to the plot by bike or car. We can only give help to a small part of each plot, and concentrate on tomatoes, celery and marrows, which suffer most in the drought.

Recently, the town council considered a plan to supply piped water to our plots. The letter from the town clerk to tenants said the estimate of the cost – at 1976 prices – was £2 a plot per year. As this was now nearly 1978 and as it made no provision for inflation, I queried its worth.

The town clerk replied that, yes, it would cost considerably more than £2 a plot, possibly as much as £4, and the charge would be the same for each plot, whether 5, 10 or 20 rods. The costings allowed for three water tanks, not standpipes, and the whole supply would be subject to the usual restrictions in time of drought. As the Anglian Water Authority imposes these restrictions every summer at the drop of a hat, at Cowpasture we would have the supply cut off just when it was most needed. Not surprisingly, we rejected the town council's proposal.

Mulching is recommended as a means of retaining moisture, but with the proviso that the material should not be put on to an already dry surface – so I find myself in a quandary. By the time a dry spell has become a long dry spell, mulching is too late. However, as a matter of routine cultivation I give the young marrow and courgette plants a thorough soaking followed by a mulch of compost. The raspberries also have a mulch of grass cuttings in the summer and pig manure in the winter.

Writing in *The Countryman* a few years ago, B. G. Furner reported on his very successful use of both organic and inorganic mulches to inhibit weed growth and reduce evaporation:

> Because it is relatively cheap, I use a great deal of straw. In late autumn I cover all the vacant ground with it, until the kitchen garden resembles a barnyard.
>
> A little straw goes a long way. Laid loosely to a depth of approximately 2in, it does not look unsightly and does not blow about.
>
> Although winter rains and snow flatten it, the soil below seldom freezes and, when the mulch is raked away in the spring, there are few weeds to be removed.
>
> During the summer I use a 2in straw mulch round blocks of sweet corn, peas, vegetable marrows, pumpkins and rhubarb.

Among other products he has used are wood shavings and black plastic sheeting – both popular techniques in the United States – sheets of newspaper pegged down, and sedge peat.

Early potatoes can be grown using black plastic sheeting, though I found this rather hazardous. The idea is that you plant the seed tubers on the surface, then cover them with 3ft wide plastic, cutting a slit in the sheeting so that the haulm will grow through. And that's it. When you come to harvest the crop simply lift the sheeting at the edge and take your pick of the potatoes, then peg the plastic sheet back into position to allow the small tubers to grow on.

But, be warned, there are snags. The sheeting must be secured thoroughly or the wind will lift it and ruin the exercise.

And the warm, moist underside of the sheeting becomes a happy hunting ground for pests of many kinds, especially slugs. Finally, because the potatoes are growing on the surface, a rich moisture-retaining compost is needed.

Mr Furner has had happier experiences with plastic sheeting, using it not only for early potatoes, but also for cabbages, cauliflowers and tomatoes. He anchors the sheeting by tucking it into 'slits in the soil'.

Mulches such as straw and peat, which decompose, help to improve the texture of the soil and add to its humus, but they have little value as plant food. A relative newcomer to the materials for mulching is pulverised pine bark, formerly a waste product of the Forestry Commission. It has the look, feel and some of the properties of peat but decomposes far less quickly, so it is useful, dug in, to give body to a light soil. Tests have shown that it takes at least five years for this product to rot down, so it will add humus for a good time to any soil, but not, of course, plant foods.

And a further warning from Mr Furner: 'Winter mulches must be removed quite early in the spring to allow the soil to warm up under the direct rays of the sun before sowing and planting time.'

As well as using soaked, shredded newspaper in the pea trench, I also put it at the bottom of the celery trench or anywhere else where this moisture belt is advantageous. If celery plants are allowed to dry out, they will either bolt or produce hollow stems quite useless for eating. I believe that crisp, nutty celery is a winter delight, whether eaten raw with a favourite cheese or braised as an accompaniment to chops or the joint. It makes an excellent soup when diced and cooked with an onion in $\frac{3}{4}$ pint of water until tender, then chopped fine and with the liquid added to $1\frac{1}{2}$oz melted margarine and 1oz of flour. The lot is then simmered for 10 minutes.

Celery is also an important ingredient of our Peasant's Soup. So I always take extra care in the raising of this crop. Bibby's Defiance is a good white trenching variety; so too is Exhibition

White. I find that a 3ft-wide trench across the 15ft plot will happily accommodate twenty-five to thirty plants and, as drought is the enemy, at the first earthing up I put a 1ft length of old garden hose by each plant and use this to direct water and liquid manure feeds to the roots.

Looking at my records for the 1976 drought I see many failures and very few successes. Perhaps the most surprising – and welcome – among the successes were the Cambridge Favourite strawberries which we started picking on 11 June and which yielded an above-average crop of unusually fine flavour. The season was shortened, however, by the exceptional heat and, subsequently, a few plants were scorched beyond saving.

Worst affected were the brassicas. Turnips and swedes failed completely. The Brussels sprouts – Peer Gynt, Fasholt and the new F1 hybrid Citadel – all produced stunted stems with only pea-sized buttons.

Germination was poor across the whole range of vegetables. A packet of Green Bush marrow produced nil germination, while Early Nantes and Dutch Flak carrots gave 20 to 25 per cent. Hurst Green Shaft and Onward peas fared badly, but Gloriosa did surprisingly well. As for potatoes, the consensus of opinion among Cowpasture growers was that Arran Pilot, as an early, and Pentland Dell, as maincrop, were the best sorts for drought conditions, although even so, total yields were down by about 50 per cent. French beans were a total failure for eating fresh, but left to mature gave a good crop of seed. Beetroots produced an average crop of medium-sized roots of above average flavour. Summer-maturing cauliflowers did well, but the autumn and winter sorts failed.

Aphids were a major menace until the arrival of unprecedented numbers of ladybirds.

In his 1969 Reith lecture, Sir Frank Fraser Darling spoke of the ecological consequences of modern technology in a brilliant and prophetic way:

WATER – A SCARCE COMMODITY

Water as a scarce commodity was never considered to be much of a problem in Britain. But the expanding demands of industry make us realise how careful we must be with it. Haphazard, unthinking pollution of rivers is something we shall soon be unable to allow. Upland water must be conserved and not used for industrial process that merely needs raw water rather than pure water.

Later he said:

Advanced technology would have been unlikely to escalate had there not been a large population to absorb it and the world population would not be what it is had not technology made it possible.

Are we confronted, therefore, with the revolting picture of the two serpents ingesting each other from the tail end? The nearer they come to what is presumed to be desired success, the more congested the picture becomes. What is going to happen? We do not know. The serpents must either unwind voluntarily, choke explosively, or wither gradually. I believe we are in this condition of the serpents, with very little time in which to take the first course.

Now there is even less time. Technology advances, unemployment grows and our society drifts towards the point of deciding that one motor car is worth more, when we share out the water, than 100,000 cabbages.

7

A SELF-SUFFICIENT FAMILY

Almost everyone at Cowpasture grows a row or two of annual flowers for cutting for the home and to give to visitors to the plot. I like to have a row of sweet peas, and a mixed row of candytuft, cornflower, zinnia and poppy, with a few dahlia tubers for autumn preceded by the blooms from a few plants of perpetual carnation.

Sam, a veteran tenant, grows exhibition-quality chrysanthemums and dahlias in a large block protected by an elaborate windproof structure that seems to do a good job of warding off the worst of the autumn gales when the blooms are at their best. With traditional bamboo canes pricing themselves out of the pensioners' market, I was glad to pass on to Sam a money-saving idea. When pruning the roses in the late autumn, save the longest straight branches. Strip the leaves off and knock off the thorns. Put the sticks away in a dry place for the winter and, come the summer, you have an excellent substitute for bamboo canes.

Here and there at Cowpasture are patches of stinging nettles, so we have the good fortune to see red admiral and tortoiseshell butterflies for which nettles are host. I have often heard that young nettles, cooked until tender in salted water, make a vitamin-rich substitute for spinach at a time in early spring when a change of vegetable is welcome. We tried this on the family and got a thumbs-down reception. The flavour was insipid and the texture fibrous and coarse.

When planning the average plot of 10 rods, those 300sq yd seem an enormous area to fill but, of course, one does not have all of the land in use all of the time. Invaluable help can be obtained from the Royal Horticultural Society's handbook *The Vegetable Garden Displayed* which gives a detailed cropping plan for a standard plot 'designed to provide a succession of vegetables through the year and to utilise the full capacity of the ground'. But, as the RHS is careful to point out, every gardener has to make adjustments to suit differing soils, location and climate and the personal tastes of the family.

The RHS plan does not include any soft fruit and is a bit on the stingy side over quantities needed to feed a family. For example, with dwarf beans the recommendation is for one 30ft row, half sown in early May, the other half in late May. When I tried this it was difficult to get a big enough picking for a meal.

Fashions in what to grow change as new subjects are introduced and are given a trial. Ten years ago no one at Cowpasture grew sweet corn; now, with strains such as F1 Polar Vee developed especially for our temperate climate, it is a popular crop, particularly with the younger gardeners.

Modern ideas in planning the plot call for closer rows and tighter planting distances within the row than those advocated by the RHS in *The Vegetable Garden Displayed*. Brussels sprouts do better, in my experience, at 1ft 6in apart each way than the 2ft 6in recommended by the RHS. Carrots can be sown in rows as close as 8in apart, while early turnips for summer use are quite happy in rows 10in apart. Onion sets can go in 6in apart in rows 1ft apart, and I give the same spacing to leeks when setting them out.

Garden swedes don't like to be crowded, and outdoor tomatoes, especially the bush types, need generous spacing. But potatoes, if grown organically, give entirely satisfactory yields when the time-honoured planting distances are pruned a bit. Earlies can be placed 10in apart in rows 2ft apart, while second earlies and maincrop can go in at 15in between tubers with the rows 2ft 6in apart.

In the belief that it is better to grow a little too much of a crop rather than too little – because the surplus can always be given to a friend – I have worked out the following self-sufficiency table for fresh vegetables for a family of two adults and three children, who all have good appetites. Each of the rows is 15ft long.

Beans,
runner: 3 double rows, 2ft apart, seeds 1ft apart.
dwarf French: 5 rows, 1ft apart, plants 6in apart.
broad: 3 rows, 1ft 6in apart, plants 1ft apart.

Beetroots:
1 row for summer salad use; 2 rows, 1ft apart, for winter storage, seedlings thinned to 4in apart.

Broccoli,
purple sprouting: 1 row of 6 plants.

Brussels sprouts:
6 rows, 1ft 6in between rows, 30 plants of early variety, 30 of late.

Cabbages,
summer-autumn: 20 to 25 heads from 2 to 3 rows, 1ft 6in apart each way.
winter: 30 heads from 3 rows, 1ft 6in apart each way.
spring greens: 3 rows, 1ft 6in apart each way.

Carrots,
early: 2 rows, 6in apart.
maincrop: 2 rows, 8in apart.

Cauliflowers,
spring: 15 heads; autumn: 12 heads; winter: 12 heads. All 2ft apart each way, except for mini-caulis.

Celery:
1 row 3ft wide with 25 to 30 plants staggered and 6 to 9in apart.

Courgettes:
6 plants, 3ft apart each way.

Kale:
4 rows, 1ft 6in apart, 1ft between plants.

Leeks:
8 rows, 1ft apart, 80 plants.

Lettuces,
cos type: 2 rows 1ft apart, sown half a row at a time for succession, thinned to 6in apart.

Marrows:
4 plants of bush type, 3ft apart.

Onions:
1lb of sets produces about 150 bulbs for placing 6in apart in rows 1ft apart.

Parsnips:
2 rows, 8in apart, 3in between plants.

Peas:
6 double rows, 3 early, 3 maincrop, 3ft between rows, 3in between seeds.

Potatoes:
7lb of seed potatoes for every 3 15ft rows produces about 50lb of earlies, and up to 80lb of second early and maincrop sorts.

Radishes:
2 rows, sown thinly like lettuce, half a row at a time for succession, 3 weeks apart, 6in between rows.

Spinach,
summer: 3 rows, 1ft between plants, 15in between rows.
winter: 3 rows, spacing as for summer.

Spring onions:
1 row, sown thinly half at a time, 3 weeks apart.

Swedes:
2 rows, plants 9in apart, rows 1ft 6in apart.

Tomatoes:
outdoor, bush type, 6 plants, 3ft apart each way; standard type, 6 plants, 2ft apart in row.

Turnips,
summer: 2 rows, 10in apart, seedlings thinned 3in apart.
winter: 2 rows, 1ft apart, seedlings thinned 4in apart.

While on the subject of quantities, this guide to some of the most commonly used materials for vegetable growing may prove useful.

Compost:
Home-made, use it as a top dressing or dig it in at the rate of a bucketful per square yard.

Growmore:
'Little and often' is the rule with this inorganic fertiliser. Not more than 2oz per square yard or 1lb per 10sq yd should be sprinkled on the surface then tickled into the soil with a fork or hoe.

Lime, hydrated:
Routine liming requires about 4oz per square yard but check, if possible, the pH level of the soil – that is, the level of hydrogen ions in the soil: pH7.0 is neutral, below 7 it is acid, above 7 it is alkaline. Potatoes and strawberries prefer a slightly acid

condition at, say, pH 6.0, while asparagus, beetroots and brassicas do better in a more alkaline soil at pH 7.0

You can check the pH level of your plot in the following way. Take a sample of soil, put it in a glass container, and mix it with a little water. Pour over it a solution of diluted hydrochloric acid – two parts of water to one of acid – and stir. If the mixture bubbles, the soil is alkaline. If it does not bubble, your plot needs lime.

A more accurate result can be obtained by using a Sudbury soil-testing kit or a pH meter; neither is expensive and both can be used many times to give precise pH readings.

Manure:
Whether stable- or pig-produced, dig in when well rotted at the rate of a heaped wheelbarrow-load every 3 rows. Thirty barrow-loads are approximately 1 ton.

Seaweed:
Dig it in wet during the late autumn and winter at the rate of a barrow-load every 4 rows.

Soot:
As a mild stimulant for potatoes, onions, leeks and celery, apply at the rate of 8oz per square yard, or as soot water – 1 quart of soot in 4 gallons of water.

We believe that talk of the convenience of owning a deep-freeze cabinet is often a euphemism for laziness. If we lived deep in the heart of the country a freezer would probably be a good investment but I suspect that nine out of ten freezers are costing their owners a fair bit of money to run – far more than the savings from bulk buying. However, although we are not at all envious of our friends' freezers, our decision to do without does mean that we have to cope with the problem of the 'hungry gap'. By late April the Brussels sprouts have finished and the spring greens are not ready for cutting. From now until the early summer is the most difficult spell for self-sufficiency in fresh vegetables.

Carrots and beetroots, stored in peat or sand, can be kept until early May. Carrots are a wonderful vegetable with more vitamin A than anything else. So I grow a lot for eating young, such as Early Nantes and Amsterdam Forcing, followed by Chantenay Redcored and, for storing, one of the Dutch 'giant' varieties such as Flak. Not to everyone's taste, these big carrots, sometimes as much as $1\frac{1}{2}$lb a root, but the flavour is exceptional and they store well. I also like to sow a couple of rows of Early Nantes in the first week of September for pulling as new carrots up to Christmas.

Beetroot is a much underrated vegetable. It is rich in niacin and vitamin C, and contains betain, a substance that is a protector against cancer. Medium-sized globe roots are preferred for winter storage. They can be eaten raw, diced, in a winter salad. Boiled, they can be served with parsley sauce as a main-course vegetable, or allowed to cool, then thinly sliced, they make a good sandwich filling with grated cheese added. Pickled in vinegar, beetroot goes well with cold meats. But a favourite way with beet is to fry the cooked slices with bacon and egg – they taste every bit as good as fried mushrooms.

The strings of onions help us through the gap and a particularly tasty recipe is onions stuffed with chopped walnuts – it is a wonderfully warming accompaniment to stewed or braised mutton on a bleak day in winter.

For two people you will need 4 medium-sized onions, 1 egg yolk, 2oz chopped walnuts, 1oz breadcrumbs and a pinch of salt. Boil the peeled onions for about 20 minutes. Take them out whole; remove the centres. Chop the centres and mix with the walnuts and breadcrumbs using the egg yolk to bind and the salt to season. Place this filling in the onions, then put them into a greased casserole dish and bake for 30 minutes in a moderate oven.

Leeks, too, are a godsend from January onwards, and people who are allergic to onions often find the more delicate flavour of the leek is a most acceptable alternative. It is a long-suffering vegetable, able to survive the most brutal treatment. Many instructors say the young leek plants should have their roots and leaves trimmed before being dumped into a dibbled hole which is then watered. If you have the time, trowel out 6in deep holes at 1ft 6in intervals in rows 1ft apart, set the leek plants in the holes with the roots spreadeagled and the leaves in line along the row, and water in thoroughly. Your reward will be stronger mature plants that touch each other, giving support and making hoeing a far easier task than when the long leaves fall about in all directions.

Earthworms seem especially fond of leek leaves, pulling the tips of the leaves into the ground where they touch, so trim back any over-long leaves and occasionally draw up soil round the stems to aid blanching.

There are many mouth-watering ways of serving leeks, but a favourite recipe was passed on to us by Richard and Kathy Brown. Allow 2 medium-sized leeks per person, trim and clean them thoroughly, and boil until tender. Wrap each leek in a slice of cooked ham and put in a greased dish. Now pour a thick white sauce over the leeks and sprinkle with grated cheese. Finish off with a layer of mashed potato and put in a moderate oven – Gas Mark 4 (350°F) – for 45 minutes. Delicious.

Hungry-gap kale was grown by cottagers before the advent of tinned and frozen foods. It is remarkably hardy and will survive bitter weather that sears everything else. But it makes for rather coarse eating and, for preference, I would have perpetual spinach which survives quite severe frosting, but is happier under cloches. When gathering spinach never cut the leaves, but pinch and pull to prevent rotting at the base, and keep the plants free of old, dying leaves.

Savoys fill the gap in the cabbage tribe between the winter sorts and spring greens. January King is the hardiest of all and is best eaten after Christmas, followed by Ormskirk Late which is far more a true savoy with deeply crinkled blue-green leaves. But we prefer the Dutch white hardy winter cabbage such as

Holland Winter White Extra Late. This is a ballhead with a large white solid heart that is excellent for use raw in coleslaw or cooked. It matures from October onwards and has the great merit that, once cut, the heads can be stored in a cool place where they will keep for sixty days and more.

Asparagus is another crop to beat the hungry gap, coming into full bearing before the start of the new pea harvest, and with help from cloches one can make very early sowings of Early Nantes carrots, Early Milan and Early Snowball turnips. But the finest way to keep the cook happy is to grow purple sprouting broccoli. This was introduced to Britain in about 1718 and we find it the hardiest and most valuable of all the green vegetables because even very young children appreciate its fine flavour. It is a good source of the B vitamins and is high in vitamin C. Half a dozen well-grown purple sprouting plants will keep a family of four provided with succulent meals from January through to May, taking over from the Brussels sprouts before the spring greens and cauliflowers are ready.

The aim is to encourage production of the purple side shoots like miniature asparagus spears. As one shoot is cut when about 6in long and showing a dense mass of purple flower buds, so two or three more appear in its place within days. Many growers take the big central flower head out first and this certainly hastens growth of the side shoots, but do not wait until the centre is the size of a small cauliflower. Cutting it at that stage would risk a major setback to the plant or a rapid bolting, with the purple shoots opening out into yellow flowers.

Purple sprouting broccoli can be treated as a perennial and provides good crops over three or four years, but it is a brassica and should be rotated to minimise the risk of clubroot. White sprouting broccoli is a rapid grower with a distinctive flavour but fewer side shoots. Nine Star Perennial is something between a sprouting and a hearting type; each plant produces nine small cauliflower heads each year for three years.

Another hungry-gap filler, if you can find a seedsman who stocks it, is Good King Henry or mercury, also a perennial.

This was once widely grown in Lincolnshire as a substitute for winter spinach. In the United States it is called lamb's quarter, in France it is *Bon Henri* or *épinard sauvage*, in Germany *Gänsefuss*, and in Italy *Bono Henrico*.

Roy Genders says, 'This is a vegetable little grown, yet so nourishing and delicious that it should be in every garden.' I have never grown it and seedsmen look blank when I ask about it, so I will pass on Mr Genders' advice.

> The seed is sown in spring in shallow drills 18in apart and in full sun and a rich soil, one containing some humus. When large enough to handle, the seedlings should be thinned to 12in apart and the plants kept thoroughly moist through summer.
>
> It will make a large clump, the succulent leaves appearing as soon as the snow and ice have left the soil and being indispensable at a time when greens are scarce.
>
> The leaves may be used either for a salad or cooked like spinach, but unlike that vegetable they do not possess what is to many, an unpleasant earthy taste.

Most of the pensioner tenants at Cowpasture are conservative in their taste for vegetables. Chippy, seventy-two, tried Good King Henry when he was a youngster; it was 'fair to middling good,' he told me, 'but a bit on the tough side'.

Chippy has farmed 20 rods at Cowpasture for forty-eight years so his opinion is one of the first sought about what crops and which varieties do best at the site. He probably works harder and puts in more hours than any of the dockers in the port, who can take home in a week's wage packet more than Chippy can put together in six weeks. In the summer he is often the first on the plots and the last to leave. He rides a thirty-year-old cycle, has never smoked, and is as tough as an ox.

When my galvanised watering can sprang a leak in the base, Chippy said, 'Don't you throw thet out, bor.' He rummaged in his hut and produced a tin of thickish paint. He poured a little into the can and told me to leave it be for a fortnight. After that 'it'll be good for another five year'. And it was.

8

OUR FINEST VEGETABLE

The EEC Common Agricultural Policy seems intent on restricting our choice in fruit and vegetables to those varieties that appeal most to the producer and not, necessarily, to the consumer. We shall end up with just three varieties of dessert apples and two or three sorts of pears, plums and strawberries. A wonderful storehouse of skill and dedication in plant breeding, extending over hundreds of years, will be cast on one side in favour of a dangerously concentrated selection. In the process the living history of our native horticulture will be axed.

Lawrence Hills at the Henry Doubleday Research Association at Bocking, Essex, is setting up a plant bank of old varieties of fruits and vegetables to try to prevent their total disappearance, and we individual gardeners should resist this bureaucratic belief that we must all conform to the doubtful standards of Brussels. One of the ways of doing this is to badger the seed merchant to supply the varieties best suited to your requirements of locality, flavour, vigour, disease-resistance, and so on.

This does not mean that we should maintain stocks of old varieties merely out of sentiment while ignoring the remarkable achievements of the present generation of plant breeders. But remember that the 'plant engineers' are looking to the needs of the commercial growers which are not always the same as those of the amateur grower. A good example is the potato. Seedsmen, generally, now stock fewer varieties than they did five years ago, and far fewer than they did ten years ago. An exception is the Perthshire firm of John McLean and Son at Crieff, who carry a stock of 150 varieties, easily the largest in Britain.

Lawrence Hills says, 'The potato is our finest vegetable, in terms of supplying the greatest value from the least space; its vitamins and minerals help digest the carbohydrates it contains and it also has a very useful supply of protein and vitamin C.' And he makes the point that, although commercially grown potatoes are not an attractive food, those grown with compost 'are a vegetable to enjoy'. Those of us who grow varieties for particular purposes, such as Desiree for baking in their jackets or Epicure for salads, know just how enjoyable and nutritious the humble spud can be. Now that the commercial grower and wholesaler must name the varieties they offer, perhaps the housewife will become more discriminating.

The following are the varieties I have tried over the years, with my personal star rating, and I am indebted to the editor of the *East Anglian Daily Times* for permission to reprint the list. Most of them I have grown in Suffolk, always organically but without irrigation and, as yield with potatoes varies with soil, season and the skill of the producer, my comments have been fair game for the critics.

Varieties with the prefix Pentland are those raised at the Scottish Plant Breeding Station at Pentlandfields, near Edinburgh. Those with the prefix Maris have come from the Cambridge Plant Breeding Institute at Maris Lane. E indicates early variety, S/E indicates the second early variety, and M maincrop.

Arran Pilot (E): A good all-rounder that crops heavily and consistently. Flavour is moderate and best when grown organically because it tends to take on a metallic flavour when grown with chemical fertilisers. Scrapes and cooks well. Can be allowed to grow on to produce firm-fleshed large tubers that will keep in store up to Christmas.****

The Bishop (M): I have tried this twice under bad conditions of drought when the yields were hardly worth picking up, but the flavour was superb. I do not recall having seen this variety on any show bench in Suffolk, but Roy Genders says of it: 'The greatest exhibition potato ever introduced, but like all those of handsome appearance or of distinctive flavour, it is a shy cropper . . . the Cox's Orange of the vegetable world'. So on his recommendation I give it ***.

Arran Comrade (M): A late-maturing round variety raised by Donald MacKelvie on Arran. Best baked in the jacket.***

Craig's Alliance (S/E): Fast-growing, white floury tubers that are good for mashing and baking but too watery for salads. Yields heavily except in a dry season.***

Desiree (M): A newish variety for British growers that is rapidly becoming the discerning housewife's favourite and is bound to overtake King Edward. It has a red skin with cream, firm flesh of excellent flavour. Good for roasting, chipping and boiling and superb when baked in the jacket. Yields heavily most years with above-average tuber size when organically grown.*****

Craig's Royal (S/E): Kidney-shaped pink potato quite popular with farmers in East Anglia. Flavour is good and tubers are firm and uniform in size with shallow eyes. Keeps reasonably well in a cool store.***

Dr McIntosh (M): An excellent variety for yield, flavour and resistance to blight. Given a good season and humus-rich soil, the Doctor will grow through to October and give a very heavy crop. The flavour is best after Christmas.****

Duke of York (E): Strictly second early, this variety was introduced by Daniels of Norwich in 1891. It has yellow flesh, shallow eyes and an excellent flavour. It scrapes readily and yields well. If allowed to grow on, it produces some hefty tubers. A good all-rounder in the kitchen.****

Epicure (E): Excellent flavour and heavy cropping are the hallmarks of this very old favourite. Scrapes poorly and yields badly in a dry season, but is a delicious new potato hot, or cold with salads.****

Golden Wonder (M): A favourite in Scotland – deservedly so for its magnificent flavour and white, floury flesh, equally good for baking and boiling. Sometimes crops poorly in dry East Anglia and supplies of seed are somewhat erratic. Even in a good year the yield is only moderate, but that flavour!*****

Great Scot (S/E): An excellent round variety with firm, white flesh when grown organically, but has a tendency to hollow heart when grown with chemical fertilisers. Resistant to drought and a heavy cropper in most soils and seasons. Superb flavour when roasted or baked in the jacket.*****

Home Guard (E): Introduced during the 1939-45 War, this is now firmly established. Along with Arran Pilot it is one of the most popular early sorts with the non-commercial grower because it does well in most districts. In hot, dry seasons the yield is poor and tuber quality suffers. Tends to break up when being boiled.***

Kerr's Pink (M): An old-timer that has stayed the course and given a good account to generation after generation of home-growers. It has a dense haulm, a pink skin and firm flesh with a good flavour especially when roasted or baked, but is also highly regarded as a chipper. Heavy yield except in a dry season. Eats best after Christmas.****

King Edward VII (M): The grand-daddy of commercial potatoes re-christened for the coronation of King Edward VII in 1902. Gives a moderate yield of large tubers that keep well unless lifted by machine. Cooking quality is moderate to poor with considerable wastage if grown fast with chemical boosters and irrigation.**

Majestic (M): Widely grown commercially in East Anglia, this yields well even in a dry season. Stores well in clamps or sacks and offers a firm, creamy flesh, good for chipping and roasting, although flavour is undistinguished.***

Maris Peer (S/E): Resists blight and scab and is a heavy cropper with floury texture of moderate flavour.***

Maris Piper (M): Well flavoured with firm, creamy flesh, but keeps only moderately well. This variety is eelworm-resistant

73

and is well worth growing where that pest is present. In most seasons the yield is heavy.***

Pentland Beauty (E): A pink-skinned early that is a real good-looker and a heavy cropper, but the beauty is only skin-deep as the flavour wins no admiration from anyone.**

Pentland Crown (M): A prolific variety which crops heavily in almost any soil and is outstanding when given humus-rich treatment. An excellent choice when only one maincrop variety is wanted as it is very versatile in the kitchen, although best for roasting and chipping.***

Pentland Dell (M): Round tubers with firm, white flesh of poor flavour except when baked in the jacket. Yields heavily even in a drought.***

Pentland Ivory (M): White floury flesh with good flavour when grown organically and particularly good for boiling. Ivory is popular with the commercial grower because it resists blight, yields heavily, stores well, and cleaned and packed for the supermarket has shelf-appeal.***

Record (M): Yellow firm flesh of outstanding flavour, equally good for roasting, baking and chipping, and flavour improves in store. Yield is moderate, falling badly in dry seasons.****

Sharpe's Express (E): A good commercial variety with poor to moderate flavour, but a heavy yield of kidney-shaped, evenly sized tubers.**

Stormont Dawn (E): White, floury flesh and a good cropper, but flavour is only moderate and we found this variety readily broke up while cooking, but some say this is the ideal potato for baking when the flavour comes through well.***

Ulster Chieftain (E): For an Ulsterman this does surprisingly well in East Anglia, giving a good yield of fine-flavoured tubers that scrape readily.***

Ulster Ensign (S/E): A handsome kidney shape with yellow skin, shallow pink eyes, and a creamy flesh. Can be lifted and eaten as an early, but bulks well if allowed to grow on when the flavour improves.***

74

In 1895 T. W. Sanders published his monumental *Encyclopaedia of Gardening* which, I believe, has been continuously in print since then. I have a fairly early edition in which he recommends giving enormous quantities of manure and fertilisers to the ground intended for potatoes; he especially recommends seaweed dug in during the autumn. Chitting is essential and this, he suggests, should be started 'early in the year'. His planting times are: earlies in February, second earlies in March, and maincrop in April. February is about six weeks earlier than today's experts recommend for early varieties but, if successful, could give the home grower a valuable crop when only imported and West Country new potatoes are about.

Chitting, that is encouraging the tubers into growth before planting, can start as soon as the seed potatoes are brought home. I always go for the best-quality certified Scotch or Ulster sorts which usually start appearing in the garden shops about mid-January, although I order from my supplier no later than the first week of December.

Successful chitting calls for a frost-free, light, airy room or shed. I lay claim to a bit of space by the window in a spare bedroom and use wooden seed boxes lined with papier-mâché egg trays to hold the tubers eye end uppermost. Deciding which is the eye end can be tricky, because there are eyes at both ends. One soon recognises, however, that there are more eyes at one end than at the opposite end, called the heel end of the spud. This is the end which was attached to the parent and there is often evidence of the umbilicus. Each of the eyes will produce a shoot and the object of chitting is to secure three or four sturdy blue-green sprouts which at planting time are about an inch long. The weaker sprouts are rubbed off.

Starting the tubers into growth in this way gives a crop three weeks earlier than that from unsprouted earlies, and a yield up to 25 per cent heavier from second earlies and maincrop varieties because of the longer growing period.

At Cowpasture the nearest I have got to a February planting

is mid-March when I managed to get 14lb of well-chitted Arran
Pilot planted over a mild, dry weekend. My method is to take
out a V-shaped trench with a spade to a depth of 6in. At 10in
intervals I put half a bucketful of compost and, if available, a
double handful of grass cuttings. The seed potato is put into
this nest after the weakest shoots have been rubbed off to leave
three or four strong ones. A handful of compost is then
sprinkled over the tuber and the trench is filled in.

A lot of the advantage of early planting was lost that year
when a mild spell in mid-March was followed by three weeks of
frost and biting east winds. However, by mid-April I had
completed planting of second earlies and maincrop.

By the end of April the Arran Pilot were showing some 6in of
haulm. On the last day of the month and quite unexpectedly we
had an overnight 6 degrees of frost that gave the potato patch
the appearance of having had a flame gun over it. Every vestige
of growth was scorched brown. Miraculously, a week later the
potatoes had produced sturdy new growth and the Arran Pilot
and Duke of York looked especially healthy.

The first lifting of the earlies was made on 13 June, about ten
days sooner than normal. I still hope for the chance to try a
February planting. Tom Robinson, who had one of the most
sheltered plots on the old part of Cowpasture, told me that one
year he planted Arran Pilot on Easter Monday and dug the first
new potatoes on Whit Monday, six weeks later.

T. A. Lowe, in *The Craft of the Cottage Garden*, says:

> Early potatoes in cottage gardens were often ready for digging
> within two months of planting and in this craft the cottagers
> always took great pride. Competition was keen and many were the
> devices used to protect the plants.
>
> Coverings of straw, litter and sometimes sacking were cunningly
> used, and some wily folks sowed their dwarf peas between every
> three rows of potatoes to act as frost and wind breaks.

The area to the west of Cowpasture includes the Suffolk
Sandlings which once grew vast quantities of carrots. John
Kirby in 1735 described this area of heath and marshland:

76

The Sandlands may be divided into marsh, arable and heathlands.

The marshland is naturally fruitful, fattening great numbers of oxen and sheep; and sometimes, when ploughed, affords the greatest crops of corn of any other land in the country. That part which is arable is in some places good for tillage and produces excellent crops of all sorts of corn.

The eighteenth-century author and Secretary to the Board of Agriculture, Arthur Young, wrote, 'This corner of Suffolk is to be recommended for practising much better husbandry than any other tract of country with which I am acquainted. Their culture of carrots . . . does them honour.' At that time farm horses ate a bushel a day of carrots and Suffolk-grown carrots were sent by barge to London for dray horses.

Throughout the Suffolk Sandlings acidity was corrected and soil structure improved by marling. This was the practice of spreading the calcium-rich crag on to the surface of the soil for ploughing in. Sugar beet and potatoes have largely replaced carrots as the main root crops of the region, though cereals account for the largest acreage, but very good carrots can still be grown here.

I gave a vegetarian acquaintance a couple of pounds of Juwarot carrots and he asked me to reassure him that they had not been grown in soil manured with animal muck or artificial fertilisers. I could truthfully answer, 'No, you don't grow good carrots that way.' In fact, I use only compost for carrots, dug in in the autumn. The compost has had pig manure as an ingredient because this speeds the breakdown of the vegetable waste, but by the time the heap is well made all the ingredients have merged into a dark brown, crumbly and mushroom-perfumed material. Root vegetables, and especially carrots and parsnips, will fork if they encounter pockets of plant food as they are growing, so chemical fertilisers, such as Growmore, should be used with care, and only after sowing. Better still, if compost is not available, is to give the carrots regular feeds with a liquid manure when the soil has already been moistened by rain.

I sprinkle a little soot in the drill before I sow carrot seed. This helps to ward off attention from the carrot fly, I believe, and also enables me to sow thinly as the pale colour of the seed contrasts with the soot.

The body needs a lot of vitamin A and carrots contain more than any other vegetable, so I rate this crop very highly. We eat them fresh from June until December then go on to the roots stored in peat to see us through until mid-March or so. Juwarot proved to be a good introduction by Thompson and Morgan who claimed it has double the vitamin A content – at 249mg per kilo – of other varieties. It is a highly coloured sort with a very sweet flavour and stores quite well.

Carrots are an essential ingredient of our Peasant's Soup, a winter meal that involves having the largest stockpot simmering gently, filled with as many vegetables as possible and some shin of beef or the leftover meat of the weekend joint diced to spoon size. This is a nourishing dish, equally good at midday or midnight, and the colder the weather the more warming this soup becomes. As a matter of interest, Margaret listed the ingredients of her stockpot and found that each steaming bowlful had lentils, split peas, pearl barley, parsnip, carrot, turnip, swede, cabbage, sprouts, celery, onion, leek, potato, tomato, spinach, a bouquet garni, braising beef and beef stock.

Carrots should never be peeled because a lot of the goodness goes with the peel. New carrots should be washed and eaten raw or cooked whole. Old carrots should be scrubbed and cut into rings or fingers before cooking.

Carrots are the perfect accompaniment to boiled beef, and are also excellent with any braised meat dish such as casseroled chicken pieces, liver or sweetbreads. Sliced in rings at the bottom of the dish, they help to absorb the juices from the meat. Carrots mix well with boiled onions, and mash well, with a walnut of butter, with turnip or swede.

In the war, as an RAF pilot, I had my share of carrots. The intention, we were told, was to improve our night vision, though this coincided with a glut of home-grown carrots that had to be shifted somehow.

A fellow flyer in the RAF, who was a prisoner in Germany for much of the war, said that carrots were the vegetable most prized by the POWs. The tops, cut off and allowed to sprout new growth, were blanched and eaten as a salad.

9

THE AIR FULL OF SONG

The most successful garden tools are usually the most humble. This is certainly the case with the crome which has been in use for centuries for ditching and dunging. At Cowpasture it is a four- or five-tined cultivator that is used primarily to break the rough-dug soil of winter into a fine tilth for spring sowing. You can't buy a crome in a hardware store or garden centre, but you can, if you know a blacksmith, have an old garden fork converted. I took a handleless four-pronged fork to the blacksmith at Kirton and he made it into a crome with the prongs at right angles to a nicely balanced 5ft ash shaft.

In use as a cultivator the crome is pulled so that the tines penetrate the soil a couple of inches. This breaks up the overwintered pan or crust, and any particularly stubborn lumps can be thwacked with the back of the crome. It is then used rake-fashion to produce a fine tilth for the seed bed or a rougher surface for the onion sets, shallots, potatoes, peas and beans. The crome is a good tool for lightly stirring the soil in summer when rain and sun put a crust on the surface, and for teasing lime, soot and granular fertiliser into the soil. In the autumn it comes into use again while tidying the plot when it functions as the ditchers used it – as an oversize rake.

Croming in late March or early April, with the sun beginning to give warmth, is a highly satisfying exercise. It is of great interest to the resident robin and the blackbirds and thrushes, who vie with each other in snapping up larvae and worms turned up by the tines.

In summertime my plot has a high population of ants. Digging up the early potatoes, I have found as many as ten colonies in a patch 15ft by 30ft. Mostly these are the little black ants, but over the past four years the reddish-brown sort, with a strong sting, have grown in numbers. Uncovering a colony on a sunny summer's day, I am always amazed at the speed with which the worker ants manage to get the eggs out of the damaging sunlight. After what, to them, must be the equivalent of a London blitz, within ten to fifteen minutes it all seems back to normal.

Ants mostly nest underground and prefer a well-drained open loam of reasonable depth so that, in autumn, they can start their downwards migration for the winter hibernation. Should the frosts become harder and harder, they go deeper and deeper. I am intrigued to know how the signal is received that spring has begun, so that dormancy may be cast off and the cycle of life resumed. It must be a highly sensitive sensory system that can receive and respond to a temperature change that will be only a small one to the ant colony a foot or more underground.

I have never been sure of the role of the ants in the micro-world of my Cowpasture plot. They may actually encourage root aphids such as the sort that feed on lettuce roots, causing wilting and death. Some observers believe the ants take small herds of aphids into hibernation with them. Ants are highly efficient distributors of seed, especially weed seeds that have aromatic oils in them or on them, and they quickly discover any fallen over-ripe fruit.

On the whole, I am happy enough to put up with the ants, but prefer the ladybirds. After mild winters and hot summers the ladybird population can build up to quite staggering numbers. Many of them die before winter comes, but as several generations are produced in a year, the survivors hibernate in big colonies or can be found singly in out-of-the-way parts of attics and in garden sheds.

During that exceptional summer of 1976 I counted ten

ladybirds to the square foot on my plot, making a population on 10 rods of some 27,000. At that time aphids had taken possession of the lettuces, tomatoes, cabbages, cauliflowers and Brussels sprouts. But within days of the ladybird invasion, the aphid hordes had been decimated and, after a fortnight, all but eliminated.

Today, organic gardeners refrain from rushing for the spray gun at the first sign of aphid attack. If matters look like getting out of control, a spray made up from 2oz of green soft soap dissolved in a gallon of hot water and allowed to cool is effective. A hard winter does more than any spray to keep the unwelcome insects in check, but it takes its toll of the birds when survival depends on food and finding a haven for the night.

H. R. Tutt, writing to *The Countryman* in 1963, told of a nest box, close to his house in Essex, during the winter of 1962:

> It is fairly certain no wrens used the box before the first blizzard on Boxing Day. On December 28 at twilight one was seen clinging to the crossbar of a window before flying into the box which was fastened to the wall near by.
>
> More followed, some flying low to the brick cornice against the window, then hopping up the wall and into the box less than a foot away; others came down the wall head first, while two or three perched on the lid of the box before going inside.
>
> On January 19, during a second blizzard . . . 19 wrens were counted before it became dark. By February 8 the first bird was arriving just after 5 p.m. and the total was 12; on the 11th it was 11, then it dropped to eight and, on the 26th, when the box was used for the last time, there were only six birds.
>
> As the thaw had already started, it is possible that two were roosting elsewhere. But, assuming 19 to have been the largest number using the box, then at least 11 and possibly 13 wrens had died during the cold spell and this in a roost on the wall of a warm house whose owners covered the box each night with a doubled sack.
>
> No corpses were found there, but on February 10 a friend who had knocked down an old drey during a squirrel drive found 25 dead wrens in it.

All birds must maintain their body temperature to live, so loss of heat during a freezing winter's night is a desperate problem for the tiny wren and our smallest bird, the goldcrest. The exceptionally hard winter of 1978-9 must have hit the goldcrest population to the point of extinction in some parts.

After a brief thaw in the first week of January, there was a week of deep frost with night temperatures down to 23°F and the days brittle cold. Then it eased a few degrees, the wind freshened and backed from east to north and we woke to a blizzard that whistled about the house all morning, left three inches or so of powdery snow, then died away.

In the afternoon, when the sensible thing was to stay by the hearth keeping the fire fed with logs, I decided, perversely, to walk to the plot to collect a cabbage for the following day. I'm glad I did. With the setting sun casting the landscape in a crimson glow, Cowpasture was transformed by the covering of snow, and the buildings of Cowpasture Farm, framed by trees, had a sharp simplicity of a Christmas card. A score of redwings were scattered about the plot where the snow was thin enough, a posse of pigeons took off from the Brussels sprouts, and there were tracks of what I took to be a dog that led to the lee of a neighbour's compost heap. There I found the half-eaten carcase of a freshly killed hare, and a closer look showed that the spoor was that of a fox.

The hare population at Cowpasture fluctuates widely, depending on the number of shoots over the adjoining fields. One year we estimated there were fifteen hares of various ages feeding on the plots. In 1977 this dropped to only a pair after some ten guns had twice shot over the stubble of the fields to the north of the site. But the rabbit population is growing. On my plot their favourite winter foods are parsley and wallflowers, but they do a lot of damage to the asparagus bed and the strawberry patch by scratching soil over their droppings. It is difficult to do a rabbit count on the plots, but there could be as many as fifty feeding on the original 12-acre site. On the verges of the Ipswich – Felixstowe road there are large colonies with a population equivalent to more than 100 to the acre.

Observers in many parts of the country have noted rabbits living above ground at the foot of hedgerows and in thickets. The mortality rate is probably higher now that many colonies forsake the protection of warrens. A rabbit seldom lives more than a year, but during that short life will have eaten up to 350lb of fresh green food.

David Griffiths, a Leicestershire farmer, writing in *The Countryman* in the summer of 1977, reported an invasion of rabbits that cleared his winter wheat 'as if sheep were grazing their way across behind an electric fence'. He continued:

> It is difficult to do much about them. Since myxomatosis many of the survivors live above ground sheltered by briars or bracken. Last year a doe had her litter under a wagon in the sheepfold.
>
> The disease has come back again and again, killing many rabbits but each time leaving a proportion seemingly immune. It could be that, living above ground, they do not have the fleas which transmit the disease.

In 1953, before the spread of myxomatosis, the rabbit population in Britain, at more than 60 million, outnumbered the human population. The Normans brought the rabbit to Britain – it was then called the coney – and great warrens were established as a source of fresh meat. And it was from France that myxomatosis came 900 years later.

Today we would not tolerate the competition for our home-grown food from an immense rabbit population, but in early-seventeenth-century Suffolk the coneys were most welcome. Norman Scarfe in *The Suffolk Landscape* quotes from *Breviary of Suffolk* written in 1603 by Robert Ryece:

> The harmless coneys which do naturally delight to make their abode here, with rich profit for all good housekeepers, whence it proceeds that there are so many warrens here in every place, which do furnish the next markets and are carried to London with no little reckoning.
>
> There is none who deem their houses well seated who have not to the same belonging a common wealth of coneys.

Cowpasture carries a resident flock of dunnocks or hedge sparrows and their high, piping song is heard all the year round. They and other gregarious birds, including tree sparrows, starlings, finches and buntings, divide their time in winter between the stubble fields and the allotments and roost in the hedges on the northern and western boundaries.

For three years a pair of magpies has nested in a lime tree at the entrance to the Grove woodland, which I pass every time I go to the plot. It is an untidy, tangled mess of a nest which appears to be used year after year with, perhaps, a modest bit of spring-cleaning in between. Gamekeepers hounded the magpie almost to extinction in East Anglia at the turn of the century, but now this shy, handsome bird is relatively commonplace, even nesting in city parks.

In May 1978 we had the second 'Cuckoo in Suffolk' survey, organised by Suffolk Ornithologists' Group, when people throughout the county were asked to note the time and place at which, on 27 May, they heard the call of the male cuckoo. And the results, when compared with those of the first survey in 1973, suggest that the cuckoo is in overall decline. On the Saturday of the survey I was working on the plot in the morning and heard a cuckoo and then saw it pass overhead – one of the 124 certainties recorded in the county.

The previous spring I had the companionship for a week of a song thrush which had either been ringed badly or had caught the ringed leg on an obstruction. The unhappy result was that the right leg had been snapped below the true knee and was hanging by the tendons. As I cromed the plot in preparation for planting early potatoes, it stayed within a few feet, eagerly snatching at worms and grubs, using its outstretched right wing to balance. How it roosted I cannot imagine and, after eight days, it disappeared, the victim presumably of a prowling cat. Since then we have seen several one-legged birds and wonder if ringing is to blame.

One of the experiences I most look forward to is a spring morning at Cowpasture when the sun is high in a clear sky and the air is full of the song of skylarks. They are with us all the year through, but are seldom heard before early February or after September, so their music is in praise of sunshine and warmth.

Suffolk must have the lowest badger population of any English county, owing perhaps to a combination of hostile factors such as the lightness of the soil over much of the county, the scarcity of the right sort of woodland habitat and a history of oppression by farmers and gamekeepers. One wishes this could be reversed because now that the badger is being exterminated in dairy-farming parts of the country, arable Suffolk might offer a sanctuary.

Tom, now seventy, Suffolk born and bred and a plotholder at Cowpasture for forty-five years, said the county's native breed of gamekeeper was a vicious opponent of almost every species of wildlife, sacrificing everything in the interests of his game birds. In the Queen's jubilee year a major scare was started in the north of the county when two canisters of cyanide fell from a gamekeeper's truck and one was believed to have got into a stream that fed a reservoir. This most deadly poison was intended for use against 'vermin', it was explained, but the accident could have had terrible consequences.

It seems that the owners of large estates, who are ultimately responsible for the actions of their gamekeepers, are a law unto themselves. Even now, punitive sentences for poaching are commonplace in rural Suffolk where magistrates' benches have been heavily loaded with landed gentry and there is still a wistful looking back at forelock-touching feudalism. Illicitly and incredibly, the torturing pole trap is still used against owls, and one still comes across gamekeepers' lines of hanging corpses of hedgehogs and weasels. It is pitiless and senseless destruction in the interests of a few people who will spend an expensive day or so in the winter trudging across stubble and blasting away at partridge and pheasant.

The sportsmanship of the huntin', shootin', fishin' fraternity was spelt out in a 1978 article in the *East Anglian Daily Times* by the paper's shooting correspondent. Having talked about the need to destroy the population of hares – 'at £4 each for export it can be quite a profitable business' – he turns to pheasants and says that February is the time 'when hand feeding pays handsome dividends'. He goes on:

> If a certain wood or other form of cover were fed regularly now, it stands to reason that when pheasants find it and other pheasants get the message that food is to be found in that place, then they will be attracted in increasing numbers.
>
> They will, in most cases, stay around that area until nesting time comes around again and there they will lay and rear their young in that vicinity to the benefit of shooters in the coming season.
>
> I proved this to my own satisfaction last year. On the shoot I rent there was one huge area near the boundary where the hedges had been removed, leaving one large field which we christened 'the prairie'.
>
> It was entirely devoid of cover except for the remains of a small pond in its centre measuring about a quarter of an acre which had become overgrown with weeds – willow herb, brambles etc.
>
> I fed this spot assiduously at the end of the season and several pheasants were attracted. When the following season came round, it provided quite a good bit of sport, but of course, the feeding must be carried out regularly. It is no good chucking a few handfuls of corn one day and not continuing the feeding process later.
>
> I was probably drawing in pheasants from my neighbour's land and if I felt any pricking of conscience on this score, I could at least feel that he had his retaliatory remedy in counter feeding.

I am no lover of pheasants when they compete for my crops, but I find the philosophy embodied in this correspondent's advice quite distasteful.

A few of the pheasants that feed on the Cowpasture allotments end up as roast dinners. Some of the older hands had the harsh upbringing and the hungry childhood of a farm labourer's cottage just after the 1914-18 War when agricultural wages were a pittance. They learned to supplement the family's meagre menus with rabbit, pheasant, partridge and wood pigeon. Their technique did not involve hand-feeding or a shotgun, and old habits die hard, though their victims die quickly and cleanly.

A pair of kestrels daily hunts the plots and, before I am aware of one of them hovering near me, there is a sudden hush among all the birds in the vicinity. Once, a young thrush, pecking over the compost heap as I sat having a breather only a few yards away, froze with its beak pointing vertically. I was reminded of a rabbit hypnotised by a stoat, and I could have moved over and taken the bird in my hand. Only its eyes moved, and I looked up and saw a kestrel hovering almost immediately overhead.

At night several barn owls quarter the plots and adjoining fields. After a period of decline they seem to be making up numbers again, at least in this part of Suffolk. Fewer derelict buildings and the use of pesticides have been blamed for the fall-off in numbers of the barn owl, but I am reasonably sure that the erosion of hedgerows, the vast increase in motor traffic and stubble burning are also responsible. Barn owls feed on mice, voles, brown rats, moles and small birds whose habitat has largely either disappeared with the wholesale slaughter of hedges in the prairie-farming policy of East Anglia or been scorched by the obscenity of post-harvest straw burning.

At a farm bordering a main road near Sudbury I saw, one summer, a quarter-mile stretch of hedgerow in flames. It was an historic hedge, at least 150 years old, but it disappeared in a few hours because of a farmer's carelessness. That late August afternoon, after a week of heatwave, the whole Suffolk sky had a hard bruised look. On every side smoke rose from fields and the air was filled with wisps of burnt straw.

The waste by burning is all the more incredible when one learns that a local stable now uses wood shavings for litter instead of straw. The shavings are from coniferous trees so the manure is made valueless as a fertiliser because the shavings contain a resin that is lethal to most plants. This is why pine needles and cones should never be added to the compost heap.

Britain is not the only straw-burning culprit: it is widely practised in the arable areas of the United States and Western

Europe. It is a labour-saving operation that is vigorously defended by the National Farmers' Union on the grounds that it is a useful husbandry practice in these days of specialist arable farms. The NFU is never very objective in its arguments in defence of the farming fraternity, but independent experts have confirmed that burning returns phosphates and potash to the soil. It also kills off eyespot spores, and helps to suppress other fungus diseases and weed seeds. But straw-burning is such a totally anti-social activity, its years must be numbered. Each season the letters to the *East Anglian Daily Times* become more vehement in protest, while those who reply in favour become fewer and lack fervour.

Straw is a valuable by-product of the cereals harvest which, apart from its traditional use as litter for stock, can be used for building board or, chopped fine, as a feed mix, or composted. It may soon be the new base material for paper making. Perhaps the days of prairie farming are numbered, too. As the supply of chemical fertilisers dries up with the decrease in oil supplies, so there will be a swing from monoculture and a return to mixed farming. As the farmer many years ago said, 'I keep the bullocks to tread the straw, to make the muck, to grow the crops to give the straw for the bullocks to tread'.

Suffolk would become a better place with more stock on its fields and fewer juggernauts on its roads. It is impossible to do more than guess the cost to wildlife of our traffic-saturated environment. The loss of habitat when building motorways and by-passes is permanent, while the toll of casualties among birds, animals and insects that dare to cross the path of man on the move grows greater yearly.

I once saw a car, driven by a young man, deliberately run over a hen blackbird and two of her fledglings that she was trying to get from the roadway and on to the pavement. When we met up with him in a pub a few miles away he was quite unabashed. 'There's too many of them bleeding sparrers about, anyway,' he said.

On the daily journey from Felixstowe to Ipswich I kept a note

for a week of the corpses on the verges and in the road. This is a
$7\frac{1}{2}$-mile stretch of the A45, part of it dual carriageway, the rest
mostly three lanes. It is, perhaps, not typical of all the main
roads because it carries a high proportion of commercial traffic
to and from Felixstowe docks. I have seen birds fly out of control
and into the path of traffic when buffeted by the slipstream from
the juggernauts.

Blackbirds outnumbered other bird victims for two reasons:
their greater numbers, and their habit of flying low across the
road from one side to the other. In this particular week, the last
of March, the toll was three cock blackbirds and one hen, two
sparrows, one cock pheasant, one barn owl, five rabbits and a
marmalade-coloured cat. At harvest time more than the usual
number of corpses can be counted as rabbits, hares and stoats
are driven from cover by the combines.

As well as the pole trap, the barbarous gin trap is still in use,
illegally, and furtively. In Ipswich in 1978 a pensioner was
prosecuted for setting a gin trap on his allotment – he caught a
hedgehog. And I recall going to my plot on a morning in
March: the rain was sheeting down, but I had to gather some
sprouting broccoli spears for lunch. The only sounds were of
the rain and the wind. Even the gulls were quiet except, I
thought, for one whose mewing sounded very near and almost
at ground level.

I pricked my ears and realised that it was not a gull, but a cat.
I found it two plots away, spreadeagled on a roll of wire netting
wedged between two sheds. It cried piteously as I neared it, and
the reason for its misery was all too evident. The drenched
creature was held tight by a rear paw in a gin trap. Fortunately,
the damage to the paw was less than the mental torment the cat
had suffered and, once released, it departed in a hissing hurry.

10

A TYRANNY OF OUR TIME

In hospital for a minor repair job, I was dismayed to discover that fresh vegetables are seldom served. This was just before Christmas when there was a good selection of greenstuff and root vegetables, but even the mashed potato came from a tin.

When visiting friends we like to take the gift of a box of our Cowpasture-grown fresh vegetables. The oohs and aahs are genuine, but one wonders if the woman of the household, often with another job apart from running the home, wishes secretly that the peas in the pod were packets for the freezer.

When the Prices Secretary visited the new Covent Garden wholesale market, one of the big retailers doing his shopping there told the minister that housewives were wasting money buying convenience foods instead of fresh produce:

'Women are working more than they did and they say they are unable to spend the time they used to in the kitchen, so they are paying out a lot more money for processed foods,' he said. 'People go into a fruit shop and prefer to buy a pound of frozen sprouts at 50p to 60p and ignore the fresh ones at 8p. The use of convenience foods has got out of all proportion and housewives are really wasting money.'

However, the minister refused to be drawn. 'It is not my job to make judgements between the right and wrong foods,' he replied.

At Home Farm, Heveningham, in the Suffolk Sandlings, farmer Fairs grows 150 acres of carrots in the ancient tradition of the area. In the year of the great drought, 1976, he sold everything he grew. The following year he had a mountain of unsold carrots. 'The canning factories only want the small top-quality carrots,' he told me. 'Larger carrots, which are still perfectly good, may have to be dumped.' Yet a few miles away, in the enormous kitchens of the Ipswich hospitals, meals for thousands were being prepared – with tinned carrots prominent on the menu. This is a waste no one can afford, even our profligate politicians.

The tyranny of our time is this sick cycle of our economic life in which millions of people work to produce goods that are basically worthless, while thousands more are employed to persuade customers to buy them. Powdered potato is an inferior food that belongs to emergencies like wars and earthquakes. But hundreds of thousands of pounds are spent on television commercials and in women's magazines to tell the housewife how superior it is to the real fresh spud.

We have, too, a fixation about road transport, sacrificing so much, so often to the juggernauts that those who challenge the need are labelled as cranks while the railways and rural bus services are starved of help.

Back in 1880 Richard Jefferies wrote, 'Those who desire to destroy our land system should look around them.' At China, for example:

> Not a particle is wasted, not a square foot of land but bears something edible. The sewage of towns is utilised, and causes crops to spring forth; every scrap of refuse manures a garden. The Chinese have attained that ideal agriculture which puts the greatest amount into the soil, takes the greatest amount out of it and wastes nothing.

Much as I admire communes and the self-sufficiency disciples of John Seymour, I am afraid that statistics are against any but a few ever having the chance to be totally self-reliant. There just isn't enough land to go round, certainly in Western Europe. But the day of the small man is returning. He represents the final unit of effort and enterprise. Tristram Beresford, writing in *The Countryman,* says of the small farmer:

> He tolerates the discipline of his calling when no one else will. Farming is, by any standards, a hard life, whether or not it is also a good one.
>
> It takes from a man more than most are prepared to give nowadays, in brain and brawn and care and hours of work.
>
> He accepts his role for reasons that few sociologists seem capable of perceiving, tied to the concepts of 'intrinsic value', such as independence or challenge, open-air life or job satisfaction. He accepts it for motives he cannot put into words, because farming is in his blood, and in his bones, and because, if he has a son, it is also a future.

When a man farms a piece of land with just hand tools, the relationship over the years becomes as intimate as marriage.

'Nothing is certain, only certain spring,' Laurence Binyon wrote. And in another poem:

> As my hand dropt a seed
> In the dibbled mould
> And my mind hurried onward
> To picture the miracle
> June should unfold.

I kneel and sow seeds in spring, letting the soil trickle through my fingers, aware that the miracle that will unfold for me is the most basic of all man's duties – providing food for his family. There are times when I feel the earth respond. With the sun giving warmth after a shower in June, the soil seems to vibrate with energy. Though self-sufficiency will remain a dream for millions, those of us with a vegetable plot can achieve a degree of it, taking the pleasure from it and accepting the responsibilities.

Richard Jefferies in *Hodge and his Masters* wrote, 'A labourer does very well with a garden; he can do very well, too, if he has an allotment in addition, provided it be not too far from home.' That applies today. It isn't worthwhile having an allotment so far from home that it involves a car journey or bus ride to tend it. Better by far to look around the neighbourhood for a garden that cannot be maintained by its owner because of age or infirmity.

Our sixteenth-century Suffolk cottage set in a 3-acre smallholding was the realisation of a dream that one day I would be able to give up my place in the rat race and become part of the self-sufficient Lacey enterprise. Cherry Place was every city dweller's vision of rural England with low-beamed ceilings, inglenook fireplaces, whitewashed walls and mellow tiled roofs. The brick-floored kitchen was the warm heart of the home with an Aga cooker that was as friendly as a smile to come down to in the morning. Returning home on a winter's evening I could see the lights of the cottage from a turn in the road more than a mile away.

One memorable winter we had a heavy snowfall a few days before Christmas, and the cottage, with the coach lanterns alight by the doors and log fires burning in the two living rooms, brought a million Christmas cards to life. It was no flash-in-the-pan white Christmas. Snowfall followed snowfall until eventually we and the rest of the village were cut off by drifts for twenty-four hours – highly dramatic, at least for our four young children. But we made our own bread and brewed our own beer, and the great stone-floored marble-shelved pantry was well stocked with food for the holiday. Outside, in the fruit store, there were six varieties of apple, and two sorts of pear, in tray upon tray, heaped to the ceiling. There were tons of logs in a barn and enough fresh vegetables in the kitchen garden to see us through a siege.

During our years at Cherry Place it was an unrelenting battle to find enough time to keep the smallholding from reverting to wilderness. But the three weeks of that white Christmas and New Year were a heaven-sent holiday with little to do except split logs.

When we bought Cherry Place it was well planted with raspberries and Careless and Leveller gooseberries on a commercial scale, together with twenty-two assorted apple trees, three ancient plum trees, two magnificent but impossibly tall pear trees, and a 40ft by 10ft steam-heated greenhouse. There were no cherry trees.

Margaret had the two children at the village school, and the other two toddlers to cope with, while I had a full-time job in Ipswich, ten miles away. So we decided against keeping livestock of any sort, at least until we had mastered the horticultural side of the holding, and we put our main effort into building up the soft fruit trade by adding strawberries to our stock. I planted several hundred Cambridge Rival, the earliest variety for East Anglia, and 150 Royal Sovereign. At Lowestoft I managed to buy a few discarded trawl nets at a knock-down price and they proved an effective deterrent to the birds. The greenhouse we filled with bought-in tomato plants.

It was a bountiful year, a spring and summer with a textbook pattern of weather: nights of gentle rain, days of calm sunshine, and everything prospered. But, of course, we were not the only soft-fruit growers to have bumper crops. The gooseberries, collected by the wholesaler in one staggering lot, sold at rock-bottom prices on a glutted market. They had cost Margaret ten hours of finger-tearing back-breaking toil, and had she been paid even a pittance for picking them, the gooseberries would have been on the debit side of the accounts.

The same was probably true of the strawberries and, later, the raspberries. But our pickers, the eldest two children with several willing school-friend volunteers, were paid in kind by allowing them to eat their fill. The strawberries sold well in Ipswich and in the village, but the raspberries had to be taken in batches to the wholesaler and we got only a third of the retail price.

The pride of our efforts was the Market King tomato crop. Grown in well-rotted pig manure and fed with manure water, the plants made exceptional sturdy growth. Commercially grown tomatoes are pulpy flavourless horrors these days, but those Cherry Place plants produced a massive crop of fruit so packed with flavour that one could eat and enjoy them like apples. There was never a shortage of customers for our tomatoes.

The soil was a typical Suffolk Sandling – dark and light and tending to be acidic. Well mucked, it grew magnificent crops of just about everything, but particularly potatoes and carrots. Because we were able to irrigate the kitchen garden, the runner beans, grown up 8ft sticks, bore prodigiously and we salted down some 30lb in an earthenware crock and finished the last of them with the cold turkey on Boxing Day.

Having tried several ways of salting the surplus runner beans, I now know that success begins with an old-fashioned crock. Ours was at least 100 years old and had been handed down from one generation to the next in Margaret's family. It had a capacity of 3 gallons and a close-fitting lid. Placed on the floor of the big, cool pantry at Cherry Place, it looked perfectly at home. This was our bean store. Whenever we picked the runners any surplus was sliced and put in the crock with a sprinkling of rock salt. By the time of the first frosts and the end of the fresh beans, our crock was brimming with salted ones. Rinsed thoroughly, then soaked for half an hour, they lost all taste of brine and, when cooked, were indistinguishable from those we ate fresh in September.

Although Cherry Place never broke our spirits it very nearly broke our backs and did little to bolster our bank balance. So, when one of the children needed twice-weekly therapy at Ipswich Hospital, the decision to sell up was virtually forced on us. For Margaret the journey to Ipswich was a twelve-hour outing because of the once-a-day bus service.

Despite its drawbacks, we have never regretted the Cherry Place era. The village school was a good one with two classes giving a more intimate relationship between pupils, teachers and parents than is possible in town schools. And education out of school in working on our acres and walking the countryside in all seasons was a bonus for our brood. Those daily lessons in caring for living things built the foundation for an attitude to life that, regrettably, is denied most city children.

The Cowpasture plot is not a substitute for the Cherry Place dream of self-sufficiency, because we are wiser now and know our limitations. I'm not worried about the price of strawberries and there's no panic about picking raspberries. If rain, snow or a touch of the ague keeps me off my plot for a few days, there will be no fears that I will never catch up with the work. Our children, now grown up, are green-fingered too. When that spell in hospital meant several weeks away from the plot, I returned to find it immaculate: the children had seen to that.

11

THE LAST OF AN OLD IDEA

November is a melancholy month for the gardener, with the year dying in mist and the smell of damp earth and smoke that barely lifts higher than the treetops. And, as the clamour towards Christmas each year grows louder and longer, I recall wistfully the quieter, simpler and in every way more satisfying pleasures of fifty years ago.

Christmas morning, and at the bottom of each pillow case, propped at the foot of each bed, would be a russet apple and an orange. Symbolic gifts they must have been because downstairs in the living room a great bowl of fruit shared honours on the sideboard with another of mixed nuts. Those gifts were the first to be put into the pillow cases, the last taken out. Quickly forgotten tokens, but the tradition lingers on; grandchildren ask, 'Why do you do it?', and the answer is evasive. It would be interesting to know, but there is no one to answer.

In our part of Essex there were traditions about food, fresh food that never saw the inside of a refrigerator and that identified the season as surely as the calendar. And the certainty that Sunday dinner was the meal of the week, requiring a full morning in the kitchen free from us. We were sent on walks and called on aunts who offered wedges of seed cake and glasses of tongue-tingling lemonade.

Sunday dinner began with a batter pudding or crisp baked suet pudding or boiled sponge pudding. Over this was poured the juice of the joint, thickened with cornflour and reinforced with stock. Then came the roast joint and garden-fresh vegetables – a little of the one, a lot of the other. And lastly, the sweet, cold and fruity in the summer, hot and filling in the other seasons.

Living in sight and smell of the sea, its food was ours in wonderful variety and cheap abundance, and was often delivered alive to the kitchen. Fat shrimps, pink or brown, were bought by the quart for salads, but mostly eaten unaccompanied, succulent mounds of them, except for brown bread and farm butter. A seagoing uncle on one of his rare visits astonished us with his appetite for shrimps. On a sun-drenched afternoon on the beach, he shelled and ate half a gallon of them as an *hors d'oeuvre* for a winkle tea.

There were crabs, conger eel and dabs, and roker or skate hanging like the ghosts of giant bats on lines in the surf, white wings fluttering. And there were shoals of silver and purple mackerel, washed ashore by autumn gales, some to be steeped in vinegar and herbs for high tea. There were baskets of still-struggling herring for baking, frying and pickling. But the best fish were those we caught ourselves on hand-lines over the side of the dinghy or, at high tide, from the breakwater: sweet-tasting flatfish, codling and whiting, all good food, fresh and free. So, too, were the blackberries in September and, later, the field mushrooms.

Mushrooms flourished, we were told, in fields where horses were pastured. Our favourite mushroom field was part of a farming uncle's land, a low-lying meadow of dark green grass, bounded on one side by a willow-lined stream and on the others by hedges of wild rose, bramble and hawthorn. It was the quarters through spring, summer and autumn of the farm's three draught horses, who ploughed, drilled, harrowed and harvested round the farming cycle. Uncle's coming they sensed half a mile away, jostling each other at the five-barred gate to catch first glimpse of him, whinnying with pleasure when they did so. There was no such greeting for us, three small children treading their dew-laden pasture for mushrooms.

Those early morning expeditions in autumn began before daybreak with cups of tea and hot, buttered rolls, then the two-.mile walk through silent lanes to the farm with empty wicker baskets chafing our cold knees. At the farmhouse the day had already been well worked into. For each of us in the snug of the kitchen there was a glass of aunt's damson wine to take the chill off the morning, and ginger biscuits against the chance of hiccoughs. Then the freedom of the fields with the sun spilling into life and a haze to hint of another mellow day – and home in triumph, the earthy smell of the mushrooms soon to merge with that of fried bacon for the day's real breakfast.

Each season had its special smells, but none are recalled more vividly than those of Christmas. Even the house, sated with cooking smells of mince pies, ham, sausage rolls, new-baked biscuits and bread, acquired a distinctive seasonal aroma. Log fires, oil lamps and a visitor's cigar mingled with the richness from the kitchen to make homecoming at Christmas unlike any other, then or now.

Now, as the standard of living goes up, so the quality of life goes down and this is never more apparent than at Christmas time. What do you give to someone who wants for nothing? The answer seems to be a solid silver Christmas card or a gold ingot on a chain or a diamond-studded collar for the pet poodle.

John Seymour wrote, 'Man was not meant to be a one-job animal. We do not thrive as parts of a machine. We are intended by nature to be diverse, to do diverse things, to have many skills.' I'm not sure about many skills. But more than one, yes. And this is, perhaps, one of the reasons why our lives have lost lustre. We no longer cultivate a natural ability to use our hands as tools. No early Briton was allowed to guide a plough until he could make one – a principle that, if restored, could benefit many of us.

Hand-crafted things have an appeal that is being rediscovered. For example, I saw hand-made sweaters on sale in a shop in London's Bond Street at almost twice the price of the machine-made equivalent. I would sooner have a hand-knitted sweater for the practical reason that it outlasts the mass-produced sort and for the aesthetic appeal of something unique.

I would sooner watch a kestrel quartering the plots at Cowpasture than watch a dozen films about bird life on TV. In the summer the pair of kestrels that hunted over Cowpasture had an eye-hurting blue backcloth of sky. A week away from Christmas there was just one hovering in the grey gloom, harried by a screaming seagull and watched by a squadron of sparrows.

So we have resolved that Christmases to come will not involve us in a frantic rush around the shops. Instead we shall give home-made gifts or subscriptions to a magazine or society of the recipient's choice.

My favourite writer on country matters, Adrian Bell, has foreseen for Margaret and me what our Christmases will be like when the last of our children has left home. And the prospect is a pleasant one. In *A Countryman's Notebook* he says:

> A feast is prepared and a few friends gather round. They are people who cultivate their gardens. We no longer attempt to set the world to rights: we are pledged to uncertainties.
>
> We may be the last of an old idea or the first of a new one. We are inoculated against the lure of abroad by TV glimpses of it.
>
> This is why we have our turkey about Twelfth Night. Christmas for us is a quiet day, a Christmas for two: we portion between us some small game bird.
>
> At our age there seems to be something more meditative than merry about Christmas Day: we spend it in diligent indolence or just plain indolence.

The time when, like the Bells, we 'portion between us some small game bird' at Christmas is yet to come. Meanwhile we insist on a fresh, not frozen, turkey or goose.

I am not surprised that roast goose is relatively unpopular. It requires a lot of attention from the cook to prevent the flesh becoming saturated with fat. But it has such a distinctive flavour that the extra effort is well rewarded. We use sage and onion stuffing and serve the roast goose with gravy made from the bird's giblets, and apple sauce.

A goose at Christmas will weigh from 10 to 14lb and the problem of roasting a bird of this size, whether turkey or goose, is that the breast becomes over-cooked while the legs and thighs are underdone. The solution is to roast for longer at a moderate heat or to remove the legs before roasting and cook them separately. Allow 20 minutes a pound at Gas Mark 4 or 350°F and, if necessary, push up the temperature a bit for the final 20 minutes to allow the breast to brown.

Roast goose produces a large quantity of fat so ensure that the roasting pan is a deep one. The aim is to keep only a minimum of fat in the pan, so every 20 minutes after the first hour of cooking, prick the bird thoroughly and pour off the fat or, better still, use a basting pump to draw it off.

Goose fat has remarkable penetrating properties, so keep a jar of it in the tool shed for easing a tight nut and bolt or a sticky screw. Country folk rubbed goose fat on aching joints and bronchial chests, a remedy that I imagine would encourage friends and neighbours to keep their distance.

12

WINDSWEPT ACRES

In a gardening magazine a reader wrote to say he had a large, ripe marrow kept from the autumn for eating early in the New Year. When he cut it open, the seeds had already begun to germinate and were showing leaves. This has not happened to me yet, but I have had young marrow plants appear in the most unlikely places. Like tomato seeds, marrow seeds seem able to survive composting and even the process that converts sewage into dried sludge.

Some writers recommend storing ripe marrows, suspended in nets in a cool place, to eat late in the year, but I think you have got to be very fond of marrow to do this twice. We found that the skin dried rock-hard, so hard in fact that it took a sharp-bladed axe to open it. The flesh was a deep yellow woody pulp which, when cooked, was almost devoid of taste.

It was the seeds from this marrow that, mixed on the compost heap with other kitchen waste, eventually gave me marrow plants in the pea trenches and among the early potatoes. They were earlier than the plants I had started in the airing cupboard and, miraculously, survived a couple of frosts in early May, so I was able to transplant five very sturdy marrow plants and had fruit from them earlier than usual.

My gardening techniques generally do not involve a conscious striving for early crops because we are quite happy to take our vegetables in season and in sequence from the plot to the kitchen. Cowpasture, being so exposed, is not the site to encourage experiments in early cropping. My personal paradise would be sited at Cowpasture, but there would be a half-acre for fruit and vegetables enclosed by a 6ft-tall mellow brick wall up which I could train peaches, nectarines and choice espalier apples and pears. Instead, we must cope with Cowpasture's windswept acres and, as individuals, make token attempts to give some protection to early salad crops, peas and tender subjects such as tomatoes, cucumbers and sweet corn.

One year I sowed a 30ft row of Kelvedon Wonder peas, as early as I dared, north–south up the western side of the plot to border the footpath. In front I sowed all my salads and several rows of carrots, a couple of rows of beetroots and, in late May, three rows of The Amateur bush tomato plants. The pea plants were well staked to give bush-like protection to the other crops from the southerly winds and, no doubt, helped to deter marauding rabbits and game birds. But I don't think the pea hedge did anything at all to speed up the crops it shielded.

Cloches are widely used at Cowpasture to give protection to seedlings in early spring, when the easterly winds can scorch tender growth, and again in late autumn and winter to ease such crops as perpetual spinach and hardy lettuce through the worst of the weather. Tunnels of polythene film, shaped and held down by U-shaped pieces of wire, are almost valueless, being too easily disturbed by strong winds. Similarly, traditional tent and barn cloches of glass are seldom seen and then only in short rows that can be well secured.

Most popular are the rigid plastic types such as Novalux, the twin-ply plastic sheeting reinforced with wire netting, or the 6ft lengths of corrugated PVC sheets which are bent to form an inverted U and held in place by stakes at each side with twine tied from stake to stake. End pieces of plastic or glass are essential. These cloches are robust enough to give good service over many years and, when not in use, can be stored flat.

The snag about battening down cloches against the wind is that unbattening for watering and weeding is such a time-consuming chore that one is apt to put off giving regular attention and in a dry spring the seedlings suffer from thirst in a hothouse atmosphere. So rather than full 15ft rows of cloches I prefer 6ft-long half-rows that can be watered from either end with a long spout on the watering can.

One year I laid an irrigation pipe in the cloches covering a row of Little Gem lettuces. This was ordinary garden hose that had seen better days and had partly perished. I blocked off one end and poured water into the end that protruded so that I could lift it waist-high. It worked like a charm, giving a gentle trickle of water to the young plants. But the following year decomposition of the pipe had reached an advanced stage so I had to scrap it.

Bell cloches and garden frames were widely used by market gardeners by the middle of the eighteenth century, as well as in the gardens of large town and country houses. When Peter Kalm, a Swedish botanist, visited London in February 1748 he noted forced crops of asparagus, radishes, turnips and cauliflowers growing in raised beds covered with glass and matting. He also recorded cabbages weighing 28lb. And in *Market Gardening* Ronald Webber says that, in 1750, the best gardens in Europe were the Neat House market gardens at Pimlico which were established in about 1310. They were irrigated with water from the Thames and manured with dung from the London streets.

The hotbed technique was far more widely used then than it is today; now, unless you live near a stable, the essential ingredient of fresh strawy horse manure is lacking. The Pimlico market gardeners used hotbeds covered by frames to raise late winter and early spring supplies of salads and herbs.

The horse dung was mixed in a heap with straw, leaves and soil and allowed to ferment for a week or so, by which time the temperature of the heap had fallen to about 75°F. The heap was then capped with a layer of soil mixed with spent manure from a previous hotbed. The bed was sown and covered with a frame, and the decomposition of the manure provided the grower with continuous, gentle heat similar to that given by today's electric-cable soil heaters.

For many years I have kept a daily record of the weather – nothing very scientific, just maximum and minimum air temperatures, rainfall, wind direction and a few words noting whether it has been frosty, foggy or a day filled with sunshine. This logging has settled several arguments about how cold the night was, or when we last had an inch of rain or a crisp and even Christmas. And it is surprising how often we see weather patterns repeated over the years.

My interest in weather, natural enough to any Briton, was given an impetus when I joined the RAF and, as a pupil pilot, had to study meteorology. Nowadays I read the isobar maps in the knowledge that their indications are still a major element in the lives of seamen, airmen and those who farm the land.

Before the advent of the Met Office and the broadcast weather forecasts, country people would confidently predict what the weather was about to become, and some of these old ideas stand the test of scientific scrutiny. For example, 'descending smoke foretells rain' is generally true because it is the pressure of moist air and wind that keeps it down. 'A halo round the moon or sun means rain within twelve hours' is also accurate if the barometer is falling as well. The halo is caused by ice clouds of a nearing warm front. Gulls resting indicate the approach of a storm because birds easily tire in the thin air of lowering pressure.

'Spider web with no one in, showery spell will soon begin' could be true, because garden spiders are incredibly clever and have the sense to get under cover before the rain starts. But more usually an empty web means that its owner was a male spider who, like most others of his kind, has ended up being eaten by one of his many mistresses.

Alexander Buchan, the Scottish meteorologist, late in the nineteenth century compared weather records for various stations in Scotland and decided there was a marked pattern of unseasonable spells of weather. These came to be called Buchan Spells. The cold ones are 7-14 February, 11-14 April, 9-14 May, 29 June - 4 July, 6-11 August, and 6-13 November. The warm spells are fewer: 12-15 July, 12-15 August and 3-14 December.

Buchan Spells may occur at something like these dates in Scotland but they do not apply in Suffolk with a frequency that would make them reliable. In Felixstowe we seem to have our own Buchan Spells and one of the most consistent is a warm spell in the latter half of December. In the period 1970–8, 10–27 December has seen night temperatures above 40°F and day temperatures above 50°F for most days in 1970, 1971, 1973, 1974 (except for 10-17 December), 1975 (except for 10-19 December) and 1977.

Perhaps the most widely known bit of folklore about the weather is that if it rains on St Swithin's Day – 15 July – it will be wet for forty days following. This is a myth, but we came near to seeing it happen in 1974 when St Swithin's Day brought gale-force winds and rain after an exceptionally dry spring. In Felixstowe, January to July 1974, the rainfall total was only 8.25in. But August and September together gave one of the wettest periods I have recorded, and the five-month total for August to December was 16.38in.

One rule-of-thumb weather guide that works for me in this part of East Anglia is that if the winter has a below-normal rainfall, then the following spring and summer will be dry too. This was devastatingly demonstrated in 1976, the year of the big drought, when the rainfall in winter was – December 1975: 1.2in; January 1976: 1.02in; February: 0.74in; March: 0.51in. That was a winter total of 3.47in against an average of 7.5in for those four months. Then, after the eight-month-long drought, September gave 5.63in of rain, October 3.52in, November 3.09in and December 1.66in, so that the year's total at 22.95in was actually slightly above average.

The exceptionally mild winter of 1974-5 produced a rash of readers' letters to the *East Anglian Daily Times* about unusual numbers of flowers in bloom. Pupils at Northgate Grammar School for Girls, in Ipswich, listed eighty-two plants they found in bloom in the first week in January. In our garden we had geraniums blooming alongside daffodils in February. No day that winter had more than two degrees of frost. We began cutting purple sprouting broccoli from Cowpasture on 19 December and the first hearted spring greens on 3 January. The first spring cauliflower, which when trimmed weighed 2lb, was cut on 5 January, a full six weeks early.

It was the mildest Christmas Day, at 52°F, since 1940, and the mildest January for fifty-two years. I remember 1975 also as the year of the artichoke. Brian, a Cowpasture neighbour, gave me a few tubers of Jerusalem artichoke to plant as a trial after I had confessed to never having grown them or even tasted them. This vegetable, *Helianthus tuberosus,* is misnamed. It is neither an artichoke nor from Jerusalem. Its home is Canada.

Today it is mostly ignored, although it is incredibly easy to grow and is said to be very nourishing. The few knobbly tubers I planted in April were put in, like potatoes, 6in deep and 1ft apart in a couple of rows 1ft 6in apart. I earthed the haulm once, at the end of May, and lifted the tubers when the tops began to die down in late October. The yield of potato-sized tubers was in the ratio of 8 to 1. Margaret washed and peeled the artichokes and baked them in a tray of fat for about 35 minutes in the middle of the oven at Gas Mark 5 (375°F). We had them with the weekend joint but the result was a total failure. Not one of the five of us rated the flavour any higher than 'different'.

Far more successful were my efforts with globe artichokes which are in another league altogether. Considering the high cost of this exquisite vegetable if you eat it in a restaurant or buy it from a greengrocer, I am surprised more people don't grow it.

To start off a patch of this handsome thistle-like plant one needs to beg suckers from a friend's mature plant or send off to a specialist grower asking for the variety Green Globe. The suckers are planted in April in well-manured soil to which chopped seaweed has been added. Planting distance is 3ft each way, which may seem over-generous for the small 9in-tall suckers. But by the second season, if the plants have been given regular feeds of manure water, they will have made bushy growth up to 3ft 6in high with arching grey-green leaves filling the entire patch.

The edible part of the plant is the head which should be cut when about the size of a teacup, while still young and tender, and before the scale-like leaves have started to open. Allow one head per person and soak them in cold, salted water for an hour. Boil in a pan of salted water for about 30 minutes or in a pressure cooker for 10 minutes, but do not over-cook. When properly cooked the leaves pull off readily.

Serve with either melted butter in a little side dish or hollandaise sauce. The scales are pulled off one by one and dipped in the butter or sauce, and the fleshy base part is drawn off through the front teeth, with the debris consigned to a side plate. This delightful exercise goes on until one reaches the heart which consists of a pithy choke under which is the true heart or *fond*. Discard the choke and enjoy the *fond*.

Having sampled the pleasures of the globe artichoke as an *hors d'oeuvre*, you will want to maintain a supply, and nothing could be easier. Aim to replace your stock as with strawberries, but on a five-yearly basis. The best plan is to replace one row at a time using suckers with a heel of the parent plant attached. Give the plants some protection in winter using straw or bracken. They also appreciate a mulch of seaweed, and a dressing of fish meal at about 3oz to the square yard in early April. After the main heads have been cut, small side heads develop and these too can be cooked and eaten, though many growers cut back the stem after the king head has been taken.

I have not met anyone who, having tasted the globe artichoke, said he heartily disliked it, but, as with asparagus, there may well be someone somewhere who would sooner eat boiled cabbage. If you are not prepared to take an untasted plunge and submit a fairly large bit of plot to this vegetable, imported supplies are available – at a price – from January onwards, while the home-grown heads are in the better greengrocers' in June.

13

PRIDE OF THE COTTAGER'S GARDEN

Just about the best friends we have ever had have been our dogs: Kara the samoyed, Pan and Karl the German shepherds, and Candy and Floss the crossbred border collies. And, apart from Kara, who was a wayward animal, each has learned to respect my efforts as a gardener.

At Cherry Place Pan was guard of the property, guardian of the children, and a gardening companion without peer. So keen was his intelligence that I once saw him chase a wild rabbit across the land and, in mid-flight, make a detour to avoid trampling down rows of seedling vegetables – an operation that lost him the rabbit, but added to my considerable admiration for him. He had a passion for Brussels sprouts, eaten raw, but they had to be thrown to him as they were picked off the plants.

Candy and Floss were brought from the Blue Cross kennels at Walton when they were eight-week-old litter sisters. They grew up into characters so different that it was difficult for people outside the family to believe they were sisters. Floss, the black and white motherly type, had the warmest good looks, the more shaggy coat and a lazy love for everything, but particularly food. In contrast, Candy, her ever-active brown and white sister, was always boss dog. Constantly alert, her eyes bright with interest, she led Floss into mischief and as quickly out again.

When Pan had to be put down he was a grand old dog and

they were still youngsters. But at nine years old Floss developed heart trouble and a chest tumour and in the autumn the sadness of a dying year was made more melancholy for having to have her put down. As Axel Munthe noted, 'To love animals as well as people enlarges one's heart and increases its capacity for suffering.'

Candy was inconsolable, her bleak misery something we had never seen before in an animal. For a week she ate nothing and became so emaciated that we thought she, too, would follow her sister. The nature of a dog's mind and its feelings and responses are still uncharted areas of our knowledge, but we talked to Candy and shared her sorrow and on the eighth day she ate a small bowl of food. She still looked for Floss on her regular walks and, coming into the house, made the same vain searches. But the brightness gradually returned to her eyes until after three weeks only the careless mention of Floss's name made her start. We believe that a dog remembers with its nose as well as its mind, having a sense of smell many times more acute than man's. So for Candy the house and garden for days after Floss's death were still alive with her smell.

All our dogs have been encouraged from puppyhood to eat vegetables both raw and cooked, but care is needed in not overdoing the amount. Juliette de Bairacli has for many years raised dogs and cats on a vegetarian diet with great success and anyone who wanted to follow suit would do well to read her books such as *Natural Rearing* or *The Complete Herbal Book for the Dog*.

There is no evidence that dogs actually need greenstuff in their diet although in the wild they would certainly ingest some from the stomachs of their prey. Dogs with digestive upsets search out couch grass to induce vomiting and they also seem to have an inborn liking for nuts, dried fruit and sometimes for fresh fruit. Floss was very fond of apples, provided they were peeled and quartered, while Candy is especially keen on peanuts. Neither liked potato in any form. At one time it was thought that potato was particularly fattening for both owners and their pets, but this has been disproved, and cooked potato can be mixed in with other foods as an alternative to cereals in the pet's diet.

Not all that long ago pet dogs and cats lived on scraps from the kitchen and, no doubt, some were undernourished. But the affluent society has changed that to a point where many pet animals in the Western world are far better fed than the people of the world's other half. A massive industry has emerged to cater for cats' and dogs' diets with dried, tinned and frozen foods in bewildering and unnecessary variety.

If it is true that man is what man eats and that the human race digs its own grave with its teeth, then many dogs are drawn into the process, living out of tin cans and with never a bone to gnaw on. From puppyhood a dog should be introduced to various foods, including small amounts of raw, grated carrot and raw, shredded cabbage, and this is particularly important when only tinned pets' meat is available. The same holds for cats, although these are far less likely to show interest in variety in their diets.

Frequently, humans have been guilty of a similar lack of interest. Before the pressure cooker came to our kitchens few British people will have enjoyed the full flavour of boiled vegetables because almost always they were overdone. Six minutes in a pressure cooker reveals, for example, that a well-frosted January King cabbage has a sweet, nutty flavour like chestnut that is quite absent when it has been boiled to a pulp.

Although our cooking techniques have changed, fashions in vegetables are far from fickle and we seem to enjoy substantially the same sorts today as they did in Roman Britain. But Rummy says we have lost the taste for onions. When he was a backus boy – back of the farmhouse at Kirton – the farmworker's midday meal was a hunk of bread with a wedge of cheese and a home-grown onion. 'That were a strong 'un, bor,' he said. 'A few bites of that and you could shut a five-barred gate at fifty yards. Now no one wants an onion that answers back.'

Rummy, a rotund 14 stone and, at seventy-five, still as tough as his leather leggings, refers to everyone of less generous proportions as 'thin as a yard of pump water'. He still uses archaic Suffolk plural words – 'peasen' for peas, 'housen' for houses and 'meezen' for mice – and 'his'n', 'her'n' and 'yor'n'. He grows the traditional savoy cabbage with an enormous girth on his 20-rod plot and says that just as the perfect accompaniment to boiled salted beef is carrots and dumplings, so savoy is the vegetable to eat with boiled salted pork, but it needs a few hard frosts to tenderise it.

Savoy is the hardiest of the cabbage tribe and now includes January King, which we used to treat as a winter cabbage. The best savoys for flavour are the small varieties and they are also more convenient for the kitchen where Rummy's 10lb monsters might outstay their welcome. As with sprouts, I allow $\frac{1}{2}$lb of prepared cabbage or savoy per adult when calculating what I need to take from the plot for the main meal of the day.

Easily the best for quality of flavour of the true savoys is Earl Dwarf Gem which produces firm, round heads of 2 to 3lb in weight. Smaller still is the quick-maturing Tom Thumb, while for those who want a larger head and top flavour F1 Savoy King is outstanding, closely followed by the varieties with the prefix Ormskirk.

If the savoy is, perhaps, one of those marginal vegetables which some people swear by while others heartily dislike it, the broad bean is definitely a non-starter with many gardeners who may have tasted it only in its frozen or tinned forms. But when it is grown organically in a well-manured patch, and eaten when young and tender, the broad bean has the sweet flavour of fresh garden peas.

At Cowpasture longpod broad beans are often sown in November to stand the winter and are eaten in late May and June. This crop has been in continuous cultivation in Britain for many hundreds of years. When the Anglo-Saxons arrived they found the most widely grown vegetables were broad beans, peas, colewort (or cabbage) and leeks. They called the kitchen garden the leek garden, and the gardener a leekward.

Today's leekwards who sow a longpod broad bean such as Aquadulce or Express in late October or early November run the risk of frost damage in February and March. This happens at about 26°F, while lower temperatures can wipe out the plants. But autumn sowing does help to deter that curse of the broad bean, the blackfly, and when the plants are about 2ft 6in tall, the top 6in should be cut off to discourage the pest further and to ensure plenty of pods. Liquid derris sprayed regularly during May will often prevent any attack turning into a plague, while nicotine spray is an effective killer for those who dislike using today's complex and costly pesticides.

Lawrence Hills's recipe for nicotine spray is to collect 4oz of filter-tip cigarette ends. Simmer for 30 minutes in a quart of water and strain. Dilute for use by adding 4 parts of water to 1 of solution, and add 1oz of soft green soap to 1 gallon of the diluted mixture. Undiluted, nicotine is a deadly poison, but used as a diluted spray it is very effective against aphids and caterpillars, while sparing ladybirds and hoverflies. Dutch growers of broad beans have an even simpler technique to combat blackfly. They grow the herb summer savory among the rows and this is said to keep the pest away.

Young broad beans are delicious with grilled chops or the roast joint, and the older beans, stripped of their skins, cooked until floury and eaten piping hot with a vinegar and mustard sauce, constitute a centuries-old Suffolk supper. Beans are a rich source of protein and a valuable food for children and adults, building antibodies to fight bacteria and viral infections. So when you are 'full of beans' you are in the pink of health.

It wasn't all that long ago that every village had a Bean King who ruled over the post-Christmas beanfeast for twelve days. In *Salmagundi* Joyce Coynyngham Green records the tradition of Twelfth Night:

> Twelfth cake, thick with fruit, nuts, spice and candied orange and lemon peel, topped with snowy icing, and decorated with

streamers, silvered laurel leaves or fancy articles of any description, lamb's wool of hot spiced wine or ale, with roasted crab apples bobbing in the white froth of beaten-up eggs which topped the liquid as it steamed in the wooden bowl; what a sight to warm the cockles of the heart on a winter's night.

The cake also contained a bean and a pea, and the finders were King Bean and Queen Marrowfat, who then set the pace for the revels of the evening, while the crab apples were taken out of the lamb's wool by the guests and eaten with a spoon, before each in turn lifted the wassail bowl to drink to the health of the assembled company.

Martial, the Roman author wrote in AD 80, 'If the pale beans bubble for you in a red earthenware pot, you can decline the dinners of sumptuous hosts.'

Eggs, meat, flour, milk, peas and beans are all good sources of protein. Most of us would sooner have a cut off the joint than a plateful of beans, but to grow meat to provide our protein intake is by far the most expensive way of doing it. Were I starting all over again, peas and beans would play an even bigger role in my cropping plan, as they did in the days of our ancestors. One could, in fact, grow varieties specifically for harvesting when mature and storing, just as my forefathers did. For this purpose the haricot bean Comtesse de Chambord is excellent. When allowed to ripen it produces a large number of pods well filled with the small white seeds which are rich in protein, carbohydrate, calcium, iron, thiamin and riboflavin.

When the haulms and pods are thoroughly dry and brittle the beans can be harvested or, if the weather turns nasty, the plants can be lifted and hung indoors to dry. To ensure that the seeds are perfectly dry, they can be spread on a tray and placed in a cool oven for a few minutes. When the beans are stored in paper bags, tied at the mouth, or in cardboard boxes with lids, they will keep through the winter. Stored in sealed jars or tins they sometimes sweat and, eventually, go mouldy.

A snag about growing haricot beans is the space needed to get enough of the seeds to see you through the hungry gap. A family of two adults and two children will want about ¾lb of beans for each meal. One 15ft row of plants will produce a little over $\frac{3}{4}$lb of dried beans. So for the winter store of, say, 12lb of beans to make fifteen meals, you will need an area of 15sq ft when the plants are grown 1ft apart each way.

Dried haricot beans should be steeped in water for at least 2 hours before cooking, but overnight soaking is not needed. Rummy's recipe involves streaky pork – about $1\frac{1}{2}$lb for a family of four – $\frac{3}{4}$lb beans, 2 tablespoonfuls dry mustard, 3 tablespoonfuls vinegar and $\frac{1}{2}$ tablespoonful black treacle.

Simmer the beans for 30 minutes, strain off the liquid and add to it the treacle, vinegar and a pinch of salt. Dice the pork and roll in the dry mustard. Put a layer of beans in a casserole dish, then a layer of pork, then another layer of beans, and so on. Finish with a layer of beans, pour on the liquid and cover with the lid. Cook in the oven set at Gas Mark 3 (325°F) for about 5 hours.

In 1974 Thompson and Morgan introduced the Fiskeby V vegetable bean which their publicity people called 'the most important new food in the history of this planet'. That was a claim that would take some living up to. They continued:

Unlike any other bean, Fiskeby V combines high protein with the same desirable anticipation of eating as the sweetest garden pea. And, one of the most important points of all, because of the breeding breakthrough achievement, it is a bean for Northern Europe, so we can grow it in our gardens confident of success.

It thrives on poor soils, takes its nitrogen from the air (no need for polluting chemical fertilisers), it is practically disease and aphid free and from a sowing in May, is ready to harvest from the end of July onwards, and it can be grown very densely. Compared with other crops like peas, corn, lettuce, cabbage, etc, it is so much more nourishing and beneficial to us per ounce, that we, of course, need to eat less to derive the benefit. So it is like meat without bones. Yet has so much more value to our bodies. It has little or no starch, so can frequently be included in diabetic diets. It is a splendid source of vitamin A, B1 and G and contains calcium, iron and phosphorous in very generous amounts.

After thousands of years of obtaining our protein (our own

personal energy source) primarily from animals (meat, milk, eggs, etc) this evolutionary breakthrough arrives. A new food source. A natural magnificent flavoured power-pack, a vegetable producing over 40 per cent of protein. It's just like having a herd of cattle in your garden.

Nothing modest about those words, and the press lapped them up. Two years later Thompson and Morgan said, 'There has perhaps never been such a controversial vegetable . . . If you are growing beans just for heavy crops and not taking vitamin and protein levels into account then the size of crop from Fiskeby V in cool summers may disappoint you.'

Fiskeby V was developed by the Swedish plant breeder Sven Holmberg in 1968 and, in my view, was released too early, before farm trials had been completed. It is a remarkable vegetable, a distinct soya variety, and quite capable, after further development, of becoming a major source of protein. But until improved strains come along, this bean will only do well in the southern and eastern parts of England when the summer is normal.

And the last word, now more restrained, from Thompson and Morgan: 'If you grow courgettes, sweet corn etc outdoors, Fiskeby V should also do well for you.'

14

A BUNCH OF CHIPPLES

The keen vegetable grower does not need to have a library of books on gardening but they tend to accumulate as one birthday follows another. I have a collection of thirty-two, some of which were my handbooks when I began the hobby of food growing as a newly-wed.

Recently I was asked by a reader of one of my pieces if I would recommend a single volume on growing vegetables that would put a beginner on the right track and stay with him as a companion while he grew in experience. And I had no hesitation. Despite the wealth of beautifully illustrated and magnificently produced guides, there is one book I value above all the others: *The Vegetable Grower's Handbook* by A. J. Simons, which was first issued as a Penguin handbook in two volumes in 1945. I bought my copy in 1948 when it was revised and became a one-volume handbook, price 2s (10p).

Arthur Simons was an amateur gardener who managed to combine a distinguished career in the Civil Service with a profound but practical interest in everything horticultural. He was a regular contributor to gardening magazines, a keen photographer and musician, a connoisseur of wines and a passionately keen motorist. His handbook is 416 pages of lucid advice on vegetable growing that is as valid and valuable today as it was when it was written.

One of the tips I learned from Arthur Simons is how to ensure a supply of fresh herbs during the winter. There's no problem with rosemary and thyme because you can go on taking leaves off the plants, and sage can be dried easily for use in stuffings for poultry. But fresh mint and parsley are so superior to the dried versions that I am glad to pass on the maestro's technique.

With mint 'the roots are lifted in November and packed in shallow boxes of compost and taken into the greenhouse where they should be kept moist and given a temperature of 60 degrees'. I have found that mint will also do well if a piece of root is planted in John Innes potting compost or Levington compost in a seed tray or flowerpot and given a windowsill position indoors. Parsley on the plot survives quite hard frosting and a root or two given cloche protection will go on growing through the winter. But in badly exposed sites, and bearing in mind that one is not to know just how hard the winter is going to be, it is worth taking a few young parsley plants and potting them up in 5in pots in the autumn. They can be kept in a cool greenhouse, a garden frame or anywhere that keeps the frost away while giving adequate light.

The other herb that is well worth keeping in production during the winter is chives which adds life to many sandwich fillings. Arthur Simons recommends lifting clumps in January, packing them a few inches apart in boxes and giving them a place in the heated greenhouse. For the small family, a clump planted in a 5in pot by the window will give a cut-and-come-again supply till April when the outdoor chives come on stream.

For those who lack facilities for overwintering fresh herbs, dried mint, sage and parsley should be home-produced because the techniques are simple. Mint for drying should be cut while it is still growing strongly in August. It can then be hung up in a bunch for drying in a spare room or attic. Better still is to dry it in a cool oven, say after the weekend roast has been taken out, or in the airing cupboard. The leaves should be brittle so that, when stripped from the stems, they are easily crushed into small fragments for storage in a screwtopped jar or the herb bank containers. Parsley and sage are dried in the same way, but select only the young leaves.

One day, I am sure, an enterprising market gardener will concentrate on providing out-of-season supplies of mint and parsley and make a good living in the process. Specialist growers of rhubarb certainly get a good return for forced sticks that come on to the market from early January onwards.

You need a variety specially developed for forcing such as Champagne, Prince Albert or Dawes Champion. Roots should be lifted in October or early November and exposed to the weather for a fortnight. If they are frosted, so much the better. Very early supplies need a greenhouse with moist soil, a humid atmosphere and a temperature of about 50°F. Usually the roots are planted under the staging in a bed of soil, then sacking is placed as a curtain hanging from the staging to ground level to keep out the light. At Cowpasture, as on most allotments, we force rhubarb by covering the crowns with boxes, old buckets and dustbins, having first given them a good dollop of manure or compost.

Dandelion and turnip tops can be forced to provide material for the winter salad. Ordinary wild dandelion plants are used although a special culinary variety can be obtained from some seedsmen. Two wooden boxes about 18in square and 6in deep are needed, and one should be filled with moist soil in November. Dig up the dandelion plant, keeping the main tap root intact, twist off the top growth and plant in the box. Place indoors or in the greenhouse and put the second box over the first to exclude light. The dandelion leaves, blanched white, are ready about six weeks after planting and very tasty they are too, with a sprinkling of lemon juice and a dash of olive oil.

Dandelion has been cultivated as a herb at least since 1440. Its leaves have a very high iron content and are rich in vitamin A. Thompson and Morgan offer a variety called Thick-Leaved Improved which, they say, has particularly fleshy tops that can be cooked and eaten like spinach. The roots can be lifted and scrubbed, dried thoroughly, then roasted in the oven until brittle. They are then pounded into a powder and you have a coffee substitute. I had dandelion coffee in France just after the end of the war: drunk black with sugar, it was passably good, but with milk it was ghastly.

The tops cut from turnips and swedes can be blanched by the same method as described for dandelions and can be eaten raw – an acquired taste – or cooked like spring greens.

Two other vegetables that are grown specifically for forcing are chicory and seakale. With chicory choose a white-leaf variety such as Brussels Witloof or Sugar Loaf. Sow the seed outdoors in June in compost-enriched soil – not manured soil – in ½in-deep drills. Thin the plants to 9in apart and by November good roots will have formed.

Lift the roots as required, say two at a time, remove the leaves just above the crown and trim back the roots to about 4in long. Pack a 5in pot with moist peat, plant the two roots in it and cover with another 5in pot. Now put the pots in a warm place, for example near a central heating radiator, but avoiding too much heat – about 60°F is ideal. The heads are ready when they are about 6in tall. Eaten raw, they have a sharp flavour of cos lettuce crossed with celery, or they can be cooked whole and served hot.

Chicory is a perennial and reasonably hardy. Roots left in the ground become bushy plants that carry very attractive blue flowers in early summer. Seakale, also a perennial, has been cultivated for centuries and used to be found growing wild on the Essex coast. Our native seakale, as distinct from seakale beet or seakale spinach, has been developed by the nurserymen and now we have an excellent variety in Lily White.

Seakale plants can be raised from a sowing of seed, but it takes two years before there is a crown strong enough for forcing. The quicker way is to beg or buy a bundle of thongs which are root cuttings from well-established plants. These are set out in March, if the ground is ready, 12in apart with the top of the thong about an inch below the surface. If the soil is like the Cowpasture plots, rich but light, then seakale will flourish. Keep the plants free of weeds and as flower stems develop cut them off. In October cut off any foliage and lift the crowns. The main root is used for forcing in exactly the same way as chicory, while the side roots are kept in a box of moist sand or peat for next year's thongs for yourself and your friends. Seakale can also be grown like celery and blanched by earthing up; you leave the plants *in situ* but cut off the heads for the kitchen.

Blanched seakale is a delicate subject with a delicate flavour that is lost by over-cooking. It can be steamed as you would marrow for 45 minutes, or 10 minutes in a pressure cooker, and served with a white sauce. Or it can be sliced thinly and served raw in a salad.

Swiss chard or seakale beet is better known on the Continent than it is in Britain, but it should be given more attention because it is versatile and easy to grow. It likes a rich soil but detests artificial fertilisers. I much prefer this rootless member of the beetroot tribe to winter spinach because, although the leaves of all the family, including spinach, contain the bitter-tasting oxalic acid, Swiss chard has far less than its colleagues. Oxalic acid is also found in lettuce and broccoli leaves in minute amounts, but there is so much of it in rhubarb leaves that it makes them poisonous to man and beast. The liquor from boiled rhubarb leaves is a potent insecticide, especially for aphids on roses.

Yet another crop well worth bringing along early is spring onions, or chipples as they used to be called in Devon. This is a magnificent word, hundreds of years old, derived from the Old French *chiboule,* and was obviously brought over with the Normans and subsequently anglicised to its present delightful form. A couple of hundred years ago spring onions were one of the crops that were forced in hotbeds made with fresh horse dung. Alas, very few of us today can get the strawy horse manure that is the vital heart of the hotbed, but one can get early spring onions, nevertheless, with a cold frame or cloches.

White Lisbon seed is sown ½in deep in August. To sow the seed thinly but evenly I get a fine tilth and, with the soil just moist enough to compact, I make a drill by laying the rake down, tines uppermost, and pressing the shaft into the soil by walking on it. The result is a firm, U-shaped drill without any air pockets that is ideal for onion seeds. I use the same technique for all other sowings requiring a shallow drill.

The seedling onions are kept unthinned but clear of weeds, and in dry spells I make sure they do not go thirsty. After a good shower and before the first frost is expected I cover the row with cloches and end pieces and leave them undisturbed until early March. Given a normal winter, one can then start pulling the sweet, mild onions to go with a hunk of cheese and a crusty piece of bread for supper.

It is not practical to have a greenhouse at Cowpasture because, apart from the difficulty of managing it, glass today is a prime target for vandals, while the newer polythene-clad structures would probably take off in the sort of winds we experience. So far, though, I have been able to keep my garden frames in good order.

Because the site is so exposed to damaging winds, I find a frame is essential for raising sprouts, cabbages, cauliflowers and leek plants, and I also like to use some space for an early crop of French Breakfast radishes. Frame is, perhaps, a pretentious word for my home-made contraptions. They are made from thick, rough timber for the walls and scrapped casement windows for the tops. But they function very well and I wouldn't be without them.

Frames are also the intermediate stage between raising the seedlings and planting out home-grown outdoor tomato plants. I raise half a dozen each of The Amateur and the classic Harbinger which is unbeatable for flavour and yield. The seeds are sown in Levington compost in a plastic seed tray and covered with a clear PVC cover which has two adjustable ventilators in the roof. Sowing time is mid-March, and the propagator goes into the airing cupboard for a week or ten days until the seedlings just break the surface. Then it comes out to a warm position near the window.

When the seedlings have made their first pair of true leaves, I prick them off into 3in pots filled with John Innes potting compost. Unless the weather is vile I put the young plants into a cold frame as soon as possible in May for hardening off. Planting out takes place in the first week in June.

The Amateur needs no staking, but like all outdoor varieties it deserves serious cultivation. The station for each plant should have been thoroughly dug out a month earlier to a depth of about 1ft 6in. At the bottom I put a layer of lawn mowings, then the hole is filled to within 2in with well-made compost from the heap to which I have added a liberal amount of chopped seaweed – many commercial growers use seaweed in this way, both as a fertiliser and as a mulch. During the month between preparing the planting stations and the day for planting out, the compost will have settled, so I top up with soil, give the site a good soaking, and put the plants out the following day.

Some of my friends at Cowpasture have their own special recipes for ensuring that their tomato plants get enough nitrogen and potash to give a good yield early enough to ripen three, possibly four, trusses. I give the plants several dressings of wood ash, saved from the winter's log fires, for its potash content, and a weekly feed of liquid manure, made from pig dung, for its nitrogen.

I put the bush Amateurs about a yard in front of the row of the standard Harbinger plants, each of which has a 4ft stake. The rows run east – west, so at the back of the Harbinger I give protection from the northerly winds with a wall of three 6ft by 3ft 6in pieces of corrugated PVC held in place by posts. As well as shielding the growing plants, this also speeds ripening of the trusses on the Harbinger plants.

When the bush plants are well established I give them a mulch of peat. This helps to prevent too rapid a loss of moisture from the soil, deters slugs and weeds, and helps to stop the fruit from being splashed during summer storms. Straw functions almost as well as the peat and is less expensive. The standard plants have a mulch of peat also. These need a twice-weekly going over to pinch out side shoots and to tie in to the stakes, using raffia, every 6in or so.

In an average summer for heat and humidity we reckon on getting up to 10lb from each of the twelve plants. Any tomatoes which have not ripened by the time of the first frost are wrapped in brown paper individually and put in a drawer at home. Gradually they turn from green to pink and can be used either fried with bacon and egg, or as an ingredient of Peasant's Soup, or in any casseroled meat dish where their fruit acids function as a tenderiser.

15

THE TESTING TIME

The best way to enjoy true leisure is not to sit and have something poured into you, but to pour yourself into something. Because my work involves a lot of sitting at a desk and churning out words, I find the best relaxation is not watching the box or reading a book, but hard, physical effort outdoors.

Ronald Benson wrote in his pamphlet *Modern Times*, 'Today with more time for leisure, re-creating leisure is more important than ever. We need to do things that make a satisfying call on our intelligence and creative ability, things which add to our self-respect and sense of individuality and which, therefore, raise our pride and self-confidence.'

Home repairs and improvements, do-it-yourself furniture making, knitting, sewing and gardening – these all require our involvement in a creative practical way, not merely as spectators. If you till a piece of soil and sow a few rows of vegetable seeds, you are making a far greater contribution to mankind's future and your own ability to survive than if you spend the same time sitting behind the wheel of a car in an exasperating attempt to get speedily from one place to another in competition with several thousand others.

Every man and woman should develop a skill beyond that required for earning a living because it could be a lifeline that will bridge the gap between entirely different modes. Even if an oil-less future brings not a return to the horse but some form of packaged solar energy, life in the year 2020 will bear very little resemblance to that of 1980. It could involve indolence undreamt-of today, with a short working week posing the terrifying prospect of too much leisure and the days empty and aimless. But it could also see a return to pre-Industrial Revolution conditions of small, self-sufficient communities in which each individual has a dignified role and to which everyone makes a contribution of personal skill.

George Ewart Evans has rendered a great service in recording many aspects of village life as it was before the coming of machines, and his books could well be the source of textbooks for the future. In *The Horse in the Furrow* he says:

> In cultivating the land man has always been compelled to adapt his methods to the type of soil, the prevailing climate and the tools he has at hand. A change in any one of these forces him eventually to change his methods, and by changing his methods to change – in a greater or lesser degree – the organisation of his farming, and finally, the community associated with it.

Although they make no claim to be self-sufficient, the tenants of the Land Settlement Association epitomise the spirit of the Israeli kibbutz and our own latter-day communes. The LSA was founded in 1934 with the charitable motive of trying to help unemployed middle-aged miners and engineering workers regain their pride in work. This was achieved by establishing groups of smallholdings, ranging from 5 to 10 acres, for intensive livestock and horticultural production. Each settlement had forty to fifty holdings with the tenants sharing administrative offices, grading and packing sheds, and some machinery, with co-operative marketing of all produce.

The settlers were carefully selected and preference was given to families whose menfolk 'had successfully cultivated allotments'. For most of them the experience must have been shattering. From the close-knit community of the northern mining towns they were uprooted and taken to the rural isolation of the embryo estates, strangers in an alien environment. After the years of mind-draining, will-sapping unemployment they were given a strong sense of purpose and hard, physical work in preparing the settlements for occupation.

However, tending an allotment is a far cry from running an intensive smallholding and nearly half of the original applicants dropped out in the first year. But the survivors founded settlements that have become well-managed profitable enterprises that adapt to the changing needs of the market place.

We have several LSA settlements in East Anglia, and one, at Newbourn, is only four miles west of Cowpasture. This has forty-eight smallholdings in a sun-trap valley covering about 400 acres. The tenants buy their seeds, fertilisers and plants collectively, run their holdings on an individual family basis, then hand over their produce for grading and packing in a central station and transport to market by the Association's own fleet of vehicles, using the highly developed marketing services and the distinctive LSA brand labels.

By the year 2020 we may have lost the motor car and with it the concept of measuring the nation's wealth by the volume of mass-produced goods manufactured. At Newbourn the holdings demonstrate the viability of the small business run as a family concern and tenants talk of their contentment with this way of life.

Contentment, which can only come with maturity but seldom does, is a quality I much admire in my friends and colleagues. It probably involves opting out of the rat race and the fight for a second or third car. It means giving back to one's work an effort and pride in achievement that can be more rewarding than money. It also means giving the housewife her rightful status so that home becomes much more than a lodging place. It requires a serenity of purpose that rates success not by the size of one's saving or spending, but by one's ability to be a provider. But there are times when that serenity takes a mauling – for example on finding a row of cloches, made airborne by a spring gale, scattered across the plots and leaving a cherished crop ravaged by the weather.

At Newbourn disaster struck the settlement on 25 March 1978. At about 5pm a 30-second hurricane-force wind ploughed a path of destruction through seven of the holdings. The damage to glasshouses and Dutch lights was put at more than £100,000, but miraculously no one was injured. Crops of lettuces and tomatoes were ruined by millions of fragments of shattered glass. Aluminium greenhouses were left twisted and wrecked beyond repair; weeks of work were lost in that horrific half-minute. When the wind scythed a path north-eastward it left acres of the Newbourn settlement up to a foot deep in splintered glass. My friend and colleague Richard Evans was there, like Margaret and me, minutes after the whirlwind struck, and we gathered eye-witness accounts.

'I was in a greenhouse with my husband,' Mrs Muriel Chapman told Richard. 'I heard a rumble which I thought was thunder. The next thing I knew a shower of glass was crashing to the floor. My husband pushed me to the ground and we lay there with glass smashing all round us. It was a terrifying experience.'

Worst hit was Mr Mark Newell: one of his six greenhouses was ruined, another severely damaged, and he lost 70,000 lettuces. 'I think it will finish me for the year,' he said. 'By the time we clear it all up it will be autumn. Picking all the glass out of the ground will take a very long time.'

Mr Eric Frost lost a greenhouse full of young tomato plants. When the wind struck he was working in a piggery. 'I came out', he said, 'to see what I can only describe as a huge 50ft-tall column which looked like a power-station chimney tearing into my greenhouses. It then roared across a field.'

Estate manager Frank Steel immediately set up an emergency centre and a corps of workers that same evening began the difficult, often dangerous, task of tidying up. A fortnight later Mr and Mrs T. J. Wilde, Mr and Mrs R. Meekings, Mr and Mrs H. M. Newell, Mr and Mrs C.

Chapman, Mr and Mrs E. L. Frost, Mr and Mrs C. Green, and Mr and Mrs H. C. Hammond, the seven smallholders whose settlements were damaged, jointly signed a letter to the editor of the *East Anglian Daily Times*. It read:

> Sir, As you reported extensively the devastation caused by the freak tornado to seven smallholders at Newbourn on March 25, we would like to use your correspondence columns to express our grateful thanks to all the members of the public as well as to our fellow growers at Newbourn and Foxash, who so generously gave their time to help us pick up some of the debris caused by the disaster.
>
> Also many thanks to the gentleman who anonymously sent a donation to one of us.
>
> We would like, at the same time, to put on record the support and help given to us by the Land Settlement Association (and the advantage of belonging to a community such as this).
>
> Our special thanks go to our manager Mr Frank Steel who, although himself on holiday, was on the spot at once and worked from Easter Sunday onwards to organise help. Without this support we would have felt completely overwhelmed.

Such is the spirit that small communities invoke to beat big problems. By the summer, Newbourn had recovered. For us at Cowpasture the problems are trivial in comparison, but there is the same eagerness to rally round a neighbouring plotholder when illness or bereavement keep him away from his allotment.

Many of the newcomers to Cowpasture arrive with high hopes that a flurry of work will fill a larder full of food and provide a surplus for the deep-freeze cabinet. Tom has had forty-two years' experience of working the Cowpasture land and has seen scores of tenants pass through the plots. Earlier in life, with a growing family to support, he farmed 40 rods and was self-sufficient in fresh vegetables. I put his age at seventy although he has that everlasting look of solid mahogany and the toughness of antique oak.

He says the plots have become far less tidy over the years owing to 'too much television and the laziness of the council in not trimming the headlands'. At one time, he said, any fine summer evening would see a hive of activity. Now there are never more than about twenty people at work on their plots after teatime and the bulk of the work is done once weekly, usually on Sunday mornings.

According to Tom, fewer families work together at anything these days – although the LSA is an honourable exception – and children are no longer encouraged to have a respect for the land and to take an interest in growing things. The turnover in plots is greater now than at any time, he believes, even though many of the plots, at 5 rods each, are only a quarter of what they were.

'With a lot of them it's a ten-day wonder. They come to Cowpasture aflush with success at getting to the top of the waiting list. Then they find a jungle because the plot's been let to go for a season. So they set to and get it cleared, sow a few bits of this and a few of that, never enough of any one thing to have a fair meal. And the weeds get a grip again, because even 5 rods need tending for more than an hour a week.

'Then it's August and the football starts up again and there he goes, off to Portman Road on Saturday afternoon. And Sunday morning it's raining. But he's paid his rent, so he holds on until October. Meantime the weeds have taken over again and all those years of rich feeding that the plot used to get are being robbed by nettles and thistles, twitch and poppies.'

He may be right. Standards certainly have changed. For instance, one plotholder uses his 5 rods to grow globe artichokes, asparagus, salsify and garlic – a choice that flies in the face of the Cowpasture traditionalists. Another planted out about a hundred or so young rose bushes and was not, to my knowledge, seen again at the site.

Sunday morning is the time, weather permitting, when we like to stroll round the boundary for a chat with other plotholders and for taking the opportunity to size up other people's crops. With so much comradeship at Cowpasture it is remarkable that there is no organised plotholders' association

131

which would enable seed and fertilisers to be bought in bulk and would provide a line of defence against bureaucracy. However, a new threat against some of the tenants could be the cause of united opposition to town hall dictatorship. It emerged from a meeting of the town council in July 1978.

'Felixstowe's Lords of the Allotments are on their way out,' said the *Felixstowe Times* on 11 August.

> These magnates will be getting their marching orders from one of their multiple allotments each year from the town council.
>
> The council decided that tenants with more than two allotment plots should be given a year's notice in October to give up one plot a year until they only have two plots.
>
> The council have done this as they have been faced with a constant demand and waiting list for the allotments.

I replied the following Friday pointing out that most of the tenants of plots of more than 10 rods are pensioners. 'Some of these men have been cultivating their plots to a very high standard for more than forty years. And they need no compulsion to give up gradually. The fact is that the local authority is trying to find scapegoats for its failure to provide enough allotment plots to meet the sudden surge in need.'

Although the number of multiple plotholders, that is with a total of more than 20 rods, is probably no more than half a dozen at each of the town's allotment sites, the principle involved is an important one. These men took on their plots at a time when the council had difficulty in letting them. One such tenant told me that he started with 20 rods in 1956 and was asked if he would take on another 20 rods the following year because so many plots were vacant. Since then he has kept to the terms of his tenancy, so it seems to me both manifestly unjust and possibly illegal to give him notice to quit.

Looked at from the point of view of those on the waiting list for a 5-rod plot, anyone with more than 10 rods might seem to be a mogul. But the answer must be for the council to acquire – as the 1922 Act insists – some of Felixstowe's many wasted acres for more allotments. Five-rod plots represent either a shallowness of thinking on the part of the council and its officers or a complete lack of understanding about vegetable growing. Plots of this size are too small to be farmed properly, that is with the correct rotation of crops to avoid a build-up of pests and diseases. A 5-rod plot cannot be made to give enough crops to keep even a couple supplied, let alone a family.

No one at Cowpasture grows anything on a commercial scale. Perhaps the last to do so was just before the war when there was a man with a pony and cart who rented the equivalent of twenty 10-rod plots. He sold his crops from his cart, doing his round in the morning and working on the land for the rest of the day.

I never knew him, but I have been told that one of the great Cowpasture characters was Lavender, whose 20-rod plot was always immaculate. A stern man, who grew magnificent crops in a secretive way, he was the first to remind newcomers of their responsibilities to other plotholders. When a newly-married young man, just back from the war, became his neighbour, Lavender confronted him.

'See this land, sonny? This is the bit I farm. I keep it fed and I keep it clean. I expect you to do the same with the plot you are now tending. No weeds, and keep your path trimmed. Then we won't fall out.'

We need a few with Lavender's spirit at Cowpasture now, then not only would the plots be kept cleaner, but the town hall clique would also be kept in check.

16

A HARD WINTER

This age of technological miracles has opened new vistas for mankind, but I can't think of many that I would regret seeing go. It makes no sense that we have the know-how to put men on the moon and the weaponry to end the world at the touch of a button, but lack the wisdom to give growing numbers of people their right to work. Even my own trade of journalism is having imposed on it a new technology that involves typing the written word by 'direct input' into a computer which then spews it on to a 'visual display terminal' for making up into a page. When one questions the need for this, leading as it must to the loss of a large number of jobs in the newspaper industry, the reply is that everyone else is doing it, so to remain competitive 'we have to as well'.

This is the insidious pressure: the one that insists we must conform to the demands of the economists and accountants. And so we surrender the remnants of our self-respect and individual skills on the altar of 'improved efficiency', which may mean bigger profits but certainly does not mean a better way of making a better product.

Driving out to Playford one February afternoon with an early touch of spring in the air, I saw council workmen trimming a hedge on common land, hacking haphazardly at the growth with billhooks. Farther on a man on a tractor was doing the job ten times as fast, slashing at the hedge with a mechanical cutter that left the remains looking like bomb damage. In both instances the centuries-old craft of the hedger had been submerged, possibly to be lost for all time, in the interests of speed and efficiency, while back at Felixstowe the dole queue grows and grows. But one must be thankful that there are still some hedgerows left. With so many thousands of miles of hedges lost for good, even the wildlife is drifting from the land.

The severe winter of 1978-9 hit the goldcrests and wrens very hard and all but wiped out the Dartford warbler. At Cowpasture the lowest air temperature was 18°F on several days in December, January and February. This scythed down the globe artichoke top growth and reduced the overwintering broad beans to brown, shrivelled waste. Some wallflower plants, and the celery and parsley, were also ruined, but the January King and Dutch white cabbages came through with only superficial damage. The spring cauliflower plants collapsed, but perked up when the milder weather arrived at the end of March, and the purple sprouting broccoli plants were unscathed.

Mealy aphids and whitefly on the Brussels sprouts were killed and I found many dead ladybirds under a bundle of pea sticks. Especially interesting was to see the way that successive hard frosts and snow coverings broke down the surface of the rough-dug parts of the plot so that, by early April, the soil needed only a light croming to make it ready for sowing.

When the frost relented and allowed us to dig out leeks and parsnips we found the flavour of both had been much improved by the frosting. For our soil The Student is the best of the shorter-rooted parsnips, although the smaller Tender and True has the better flavour. February is the traditional sowing time because the parsnip needs a long growing season. But I always get better germination by waiting until late March or early April. Then I make station sowings of three seeds at 3in intervals and thin out to one plant per station. Closer spacing than the generally recommended 6in apart helps to prevent canker which is endemic on our plots. As parsnip seed takes up to thirty days to germinate, I mark the rows for hand-weeding by sowing radish seed in between the parsnip stations.

Some growers take great pride in producing long white roots for exhibition and about the only way of ensuring show-quality specimens is to sow the seed in specially prepared positions. This means making holes 2ft deep and 4in or so in diameter and filling them with sieved compost or a mixture of sand and peat. Three seeds are sown in each hole and thinned to one strong plant. To get the roots out without damage calls for great care and it is usual to dig a trench alongside the chosen roots and take them out sideways. White Gem is a good variety for show purposes and it has a pretty good resistance to canker.

While parsnips are a tasty ingredient of winter stews, we reckon that plain, boiled parsnip is the dullest of all vegetables. But baked or roast parsnip is delicious and very simply prepared by quartering the roots lengthways and removing the core. The fingers of parsnip are put in with the joint or parboiled and baked in a well-greased covered dish for about 1½ hours in a moderate oven.

Another root vegetable which is a godsend from January onwards is the swede, originally the Swedish turnip, which arrived in England from Holland in 1755. Devon growers produce fine specimens weighing up to 4lb per root with a delicate flavour less harsh than that of the turnip. Both swedes and turnips are brassicas so I always include them in the rotation plan for the greens.

At Cowpasture swedes fail more often than any other crop; this is usually due either to parched conditions in the early life of the plant, sowing too late or too soon, or attack by the turnip flea beetle. Because of these factors and the relative cheapness of commercially grown swedes, probably not more than a third of the plotholders bother with the crop.

I make two sowings of the variety Purple-Top Improved, which has orange flesh, a purple skin and a sweet, mild flavour. This crop needs up to six months to grow to full size, but an early sowing in late March or April will give cricket-ball-sized roots for eating in the early autumn. The maincrop sowing I make in May after the soil has had a good shower of rain. I leave the roots in the ground over the winter, taking a root at a time home to the cook.

Swedes will not succeed if they are crowded. They relish an open site with plenty of air movement, so they are a good subject to put at the north end of the brassica patch. To prevent the flea beetle attacking the seedlings, I give them a thorough dusting with derris. Swede, mashed with a walnut of butter, is a good dish-mate to lamb chops or steak and a prime ingredient of Peasant's Soup. But with roast, braised or boiled rabbit it makes a meal for the gourmet.

Turnips are another problem crop in our dry part of the country and, while seldom clocking up the failure rate of swedes, the roots become fibrous, even woody, in a drought. Given adequate moisture, turnips respond to Cowpasture's richness, where compost, pig manure and seaweed have been fed to the soil year upon year. I grow the handsome flat-topped purple and white Early Milan for the first sowings, treating it like a salad crop by sowing half a row at a time. I make four sowings at fortnightly intervals beginning, if all is well, in the first week of April. The two rows are 10in apart and I thin the seedlings to 3in apart.

With these spring sowings the aim is to get the seedlings moving briskly to maturity so that the roots from the first sowing in early April are ready at the end of May. Early Milan should be pulled when young and tender at about the size of a tennis ball and I find that the half-row of 7ft 6in is enough to give a family of four or five three good servings.

The two rows for winter use are sown in late July or early August using the variety Golden Ball. As the name suggests, this is not a white-fleshed kind. It has an attractive butter-coloured flesh and the flavour is slightly stronger than that of swede. Overwintered turnips are not so hardy as swedes, so I lift the remains of the crop in December, cut off the tap roots and the remnants of the leaves and stalks and put the roots in a box of peat.

137

Some Cowpasture growers allow their turnips to remain undisturbed through the winter so that in April they can cut the new top growth for use as a green vegetable. Turnip greens have the pleasant bitterness of spinach and are rich in vitamin C. My grandmother drank the liquor that turnip tops had been boiled in and she swore that it helped keep rheumatism at bay.

Eddie says rheumatism comes easily to him and stays as long as an unwelcome mother-in-law. The seeds were sown, he told me, when he walked a coal cart through the villages, getting soaked to the skin in the process. Now, at seventy-four, and despite arthritic joints and rheumatism, he keeps his plot immaculate.

When I felt the first twinges in my hands there was a wave of panic. I earn my living with my hands, by writing, and I grow food with them. If they were to become stiff and twisted, life would be very difficult. So it was a relief to be told that I had that music-hall joke of a complaint, gout, which responds quite well to modern drugs. The mystery is how this disease strikes, because compared to the port-drinking face-stuffing victims of Edwardian times, I lead a spartan life. However, the pain is no laughing matter.

Celery is said to be particularly good for relieving rheumatism; so, too, are leeks, tomatoes and asparagus. The gypsy recipe is to eat plenty of cooked young stinging nettles which, because nettles are alkaline, are said to be a solvent of uric acid, the substance that also causes the gout inflammation. The Romans drank the liquor in which couch-grass roots had been boiled. Yet another remedy was given to me by a vet. You boil 1oz of dandelion root in $1\frac{1}{2}$ pints of rainwater for half an hour. Strain and bottle the liquid and take a wineglassful twice a day. And Eddie said that his father used a good old Suffolk recipe to keep rheumatic pains out of his feet. Every night when he went to bed he took off his socks and placed them in the form of a cross at the foot of the bed.

For people with an electric juice extractor, I have been told that the most health-giving drink is obtained from a mixture of carrots, spinach and celery in equal proportions and a teaspoonful of chopped parsley. Carotene, the yellow pigment in carrots, is converted in the body to vitamin A and stored in the liver; it helps to relieve acidity and anaemia. Celery juice, as well as fighting rheumatism, is said to lower high blood pressure, while spinach juice is good for both anaemia and the complexion.

If everyone ate onions, no one would find it objectionable. But the age-old way of disguising one's onion-laden breath is to chew a sprig of parsley, which is rich in chlorophyll. It is also a valuable source of iron, calcium and trace elements. Paul Fournier says of parsley, 'One may, without exaggeration, consider it as one of the most valuable health-giving foodstuffs that Nature has generously put at the disposal of mankind.'

It is said that parsley will only germinate if sown by an upright and honest man. If you don't qualify, try soaking the seed in water for twenty-four hours before sowing, and expect to wait five weeks or more before the seedlings appear.

The double curled varieties are the most attractive, and Moss Curled Extra Triple is well worth seeking out. A few years ago this variety was listed in the catalogue of one of our largest retail seedsmen, so I went to the local branch and asked for it. 'All we've got is plain parsley,' said the plainly bored sales assistant, 'don't know anything about curled stuff.' In contrast, a visit to Notcutts at Woodbridge is always a pleasure, every inquiry being met with courtesy and answered with confidence.

In 1978, after a cold spring foreshadowing the rather more severe one of the following year, late May and early June gave rainless weeks, and veterans were predicting a return of the 1976 drought. But the last ten days of June brought rain every day. On 5 July we had notched up fifteen days of consecutive rainfall with barely a sight of the sun. Temperatures frequently dropped by as much as 20°F below the average and the cause, paradoxically, was a weather pattern similar to that in the hot, dry summer of 1976.

A semi-permanent high-pressure area in the region of the

Azores normally builds a ridge that pushes towards Britain in June and July. This keeps the low-pressure cyclonic depressions to the north and east and allows a succession of warm, sunny days to become established over the British Isles. In 1978 the anticyclone was 1,000 miles south-west of Britain – too far away to allow its influence to be felt – and so we were bombarded by one depression after another moving clockwise round the island, bringing rain and, to the eastern side of the country, northerly winds.

Rainfall amounts varied greatly, with the north and west getting the biggest totals. At Cowpasture the record for this exceptionally dull, wet spell was: June 21, 0.16in; 22, 0.12; 23, 0.25; 24, trace; 25, 0.11; 26, 0.03; 27, 0.05; 28, 0.16; 29, 0.08; 30, 0.07; July 1, 0.05; 2, 0.07; 3, 0.02; 4, 0.26; 5, 0.03. This is a total for the fifteen days of 1.46in, against more than 3in in parts of the west, and 1.53in in central Ipswich.

This spell brought some loss of strawberries due to botrytis or grey mould. We started picking from our patch on 23 June and managed to gather some every day in between showers. The yield was average, even though the slugs had an above-average fill. The maximum yield, I find, in any but an abnormally dry season occurs about a fortnight after picking begins, and then it tails off fairly abruptly.

After the dull, wet spell, the rest of July was given over to a typical anticyclonic pattern of warm, dry but not particularly sunny days.

It is difficult for the newcomer to soft-fruit growing to appreciate that the crop must be picked as it ripens, so holidays away are better avoided during the peak of the season. Sometimes, too, the yields can provide a surfeit that is embarrassing unless one plans in advance to fill the freezer, make jam or delight one's friends with the surplus. So it might be interesting to record the daily score from my patch in a fairly typical season.

The picking went like this from eight rows, each of ten plants, made up of four rows of three-year-old plants, two of two-year-old, and two rows of maidens: June 23, 5½lb; 26, 3lb; 30, 5lb; July 1, 3lb; 3, 6lb; 5, 3lb; 8, 3½lb; 9, 1½lb; 10, 8lb; 12, 6½lb; 13, 9lb; 16, 7lb; 18, 4½lb; 20, 3lb; 21, 2½lb; 23, 3lb. A total of 74lb.

Another phenomenon of the sodden conditions was the keeling over of young brassica plants. They made vigorous top growth and, apparently, a mass of fibrous roots but not the stronger tap root system. So in a stiffish wind they had little anchorage and readily tipped over. Brussels sprouts and cauliflowers especially resent this check to their growth and often turn in open-buttoned sprouts and blind heads.

Bob, a veteran grower of prizewinning sprouts, has a technique that is unusual but highly successful. On his brassica plot he sows a few seeds of Brussels at the stations where the plants will mature. As the seedlings develop, he thins all but the strongest plant so from seedling to maturity there is no transplanting and so no check to growth.

The cold, wet spring caused very patchy germination of some crops. Kelvedon Wonder and Hurst Green Shaft peas struggled to produce about one plant from every six seeds sown and there were also the usual losses to mice and birds. A total of six rows sown in late April and early May had made only about 6in of growth by mid-June and there were wide gaps everywhere. So I sowed more seed in the gaps and hoped Nature would do her customary balancing act. I was not disappointed. By mid-July, when the first pickings were made from the Kelvedon Wonder, the later-sown seed had grown taller plants than the earlier ones, but the pods were about ten to fourteen days behind. So the picking period was extended in a very useful way.

A dry, warm period from mid-July to early August gave the Hurst Green Shaft a boost and the flavour, normally excellent, was accentuated. Then came another spell of cool, wet days which suited the French beans and the runners and the winter greenstuff. On balance, vegetable growers prefer cool, wet summers to the hot, drought-stricken weeks of a normal Felixstowe summer, but of course the holiday trade takes a battering.

Bad germination is a feature of cold, wet springs. My neighbour Frank had no success at all with parsnips. Delayed because of the weather, his sowing of two rows in late April produced nothing, not even a solitary seedling. And, because of the customary slow germination of parsnips, by the time he realised the sowing had failed, it was too late to have another go.

Perhaps the biggest lesson from gardening at Cowpasture is that one seldom learns from experience because conditions are never identical. That strange summer of 1978, alternating between cool, wet spells and long periods with drying winds and nil rainfall, gave one of the most difficult seasons for the Cowpasture growers. Almost every crop gave well below average yields with the one exception of the maincrop potatoes. Here we had outstanding successes with all the most popular varieties, while those who grew Pentland Crown lifted a phenomenal weight of well-finished tubers, many of which weighed more than a pound each.

But the weather did not suit outdoor tomatoes. Looking at the unripe trusses on my plot, I remembered a tip from way back. So I cut a sackful of nettles to put in a 3ft-cube-size box along with the green tomatoes. It worked like a charm. In a fortnight to three weeks they ripened well – far better than by the more usual method of wrapping them in brown paper, putting them in a drawer and then, all too often, forgetting about them.

The nettle is still widely used in homoeopathy. Nettle tea is said to be particularly valuable in the treatment of anaemia, rheumatism and enteritis. Country people use the seeds in several ways for various remedies. As an aphrodisiac, half a teaspoonful of nettle seeds taken in honey is recommended. And nettle juice, used as a scalp massage, is reckoned to be effective against dandruff and to encourage a thick, healthy head of hair. But why nettles are able to ripen tomatoes is a mystery. So also was the emergence of an Italian plum-type tomato among my home-raised Harbinger.

The seed was bought fresh from one of the big suppliers and I raised twenty plants for the greenhouse and for outdoors on the plot. They came on reasonably well in that indifferent season, but it was only when the first trusses began to form that I realised one of the six greenhouse plants was a sport. Eventually the fruit ripened to a magnificent deep crimson and the shape was a true plum, each about 4in from top to bottom and with a girth of about 6in. However, the flesh was pithy and the flavour insipid, so I wasted one-sixth of my time and effort on raising a very handsome foreigner whose performance at the table left a lot to be desired.

To set against that disappointment was the discovery of Romano, whose promise was fulsome. Romano is a new climbing French bean from Thompson and Morgan who claimed, 'As soon as you taste this bean you will be astonished at its distinct mouth-watering flavour, far superior to other varieties. It is fleshy, meaty, stringless and snaps easily. Freeze it, if you can, to remind you of its outstanding flavour.'

I sowed the seeds in late April, 12in apart, 3in deep, with the rows 3ft apart. The plants were trained up 6ft-tall bamboo canes, crossed and tied at the top in an inverted V. The young plants were readily teased away from the canes by wind, so I loosely tied them with raffia. I found, too, that a mulch of grass cuttings applied after a good shower was much appreciated.

A small packet of about two dozen seeds cost 49p, but germination was good, the yield was fairly high, and the flavour remarkable. Coming before the runner beans but after the peas, Romano deserves to become a family favourite. The beans are at their very best when picked young, that is about 6in long. They need very little attention in the kitchen, just a brisk topping and tailing, then into the saucepan of boiling, salted water for 15 minutes or the pressure cooker for 5 minutes.

I didn't weigh the maincrop potato yield for that summer of 1978, but I reckon that 14lb of Desiree seed and 14lb of Pentland Crown jointly gave 300lb of superb-quality spuds. Crown outcropped Desiree by about 70 per cent. One haulm gave seven tubers each weighing $1\frac{1}{4}$lb, although the flavour is well behind the five-star quality of Desiree.

Some Cowpasture growers still use King Edward as their maincrop, and on the humus-rich plots in a wettish season this old-timer looks splendid. 'My old girl has been peeling King Edwards for half a century,' said Sam. 'She don't want to change now.' But most of the younger tenants are willing to experiment and I've seen some fine crops of Maris Piper and the three Pentland maincrops, Dell, Ivory and Crown. One of the newcomers used Maris Peer as his early crop, and Maris Piper for maincrop, arguing that as they were raised in Cambridge, they must be well suited to East Anglian conditions. This may be so in terms of ability to withstand drought, but the soils at Cowpasture and Cambridge are quite different.

The St Luke's summer of 1978, giving an almost rain-free period through September, October and much of November, proved more damaging for winter brassicas than the drought of 1976, but the grain harvest was a record $17\frac{1}{2}$ million tonnes.

The autumn drought took a big toll of shrew-mice. They catch worms on the surface or just underground, but in the drought there were few worms to be had and so many of Cowpasture's shrews died of starvation. But if the corpses of shrew-mice are a saddening sight, a glimpse of a resident weasel in a bank of nettles near my plot was a delightful surprise. The brilliant white throat and chest showed off to perfection the chestnut fur on the back and the button-bright eyes. I have seen at dawn a family of weasels, mother and three youngsters, hunting in the grass alongside the northern hedge at Cowpasture. But the lone weasel, standing sniffing the air within a few yards of my plot, was a most welcome sight. It meant, I trust, less chance of my compost heap becoming home with a built-in restaurant to the rats in the winter ahead.

If 1976 was the year of the ladybird, 1978 was the year of the daddy-long-legs. These are the crane-flies which some summers come into the garden and house in great numbers. The larvae of these flies are, of course, the infamous leatherjackets which can do so much damage in the vegetable plot.

That Indian summer I will remember for the charms of goldfinches that haunted Cowpasture. Families constantly flitted to uncultivated plots to feed on the seed heads of thistles, and how perfectly the golden tints of autumn were reflected in the hues of their feathers. In Victorian times this bird was trapped and caged for its tinkling song. The Royal Society for the Protection of Birds made the saving of the goldfinch from the bird limer one of its first tasks after it was founded in 1889.

The RSPB, with a membership close to 250,000, has more members than any other conservation organisation in Britain. And now, perversely, the threat to the wellbeing of many bird colonies comes not from nest robbers and bird trappers, but from the sheer pressure of numbers of people in pursuit of leisure. Fortunately, the Society's own bird reserves are very carefully managed to avoid over-stressing the wildlife.

17

RAIN-SODDEN HOURS

Now, with the long haul of winter ahead, one can face it with optimism. In the cellar there are ten strings of onions and five sacks of potatoes. There are boxes of peat with layers of carrots and beetroots nestling in them, and also safely gathered in are swedes and parsnips and the last of the tomatoes.

It may be the instinct of a squirrel, but the need to prepare for the bleak days ahead comes through very strongly in late October. Fortunately, this Victorian house has cellars the size of a small bungalow so storage space is no problem. There are 40 bushels of logs, stacked from floor to ceiling, a couple of tons of coal for the living-room fire, and about 5 tons of anthracite beans to fuel the boiler. Elsewhere in the cellar are shelves of home-made beer and wines and jars of pickled onions and red cabbage. There are pots of hyacinths waiting to be brought up later, to give the dreariest days of winter a sight and smell of spring.

Now that the first frost of winter has cut them down, the dahlias from Cowpasture have ended their three-month task of providing flowers for the home and have gone into store in the dry, cool cellar. They were individually labelled, thoroughly dried, dusted with flowers of sulphur and finally packed into a box of dry peat.

There is a fairly wide variation over the years on the timing of the first frost of autumn. The earliest first frost and the latest spring frost over the eight years 1971-8 came during the winter of 1974-5. Great contrasts in weather characterised 1974. It gave an above-average rainfall of 24.63in, but the driest spring for 100 years, when the total rain for the first six months was only 6.26in. There were above-average gales from August onwards. Then came the coldest autumn for forty years, followed by the mildest Christmas Day, at 52°F since 1940.

The table looks like this:

	First frost	Last frost
1971–2	Nov 6	March 1
1972–3	Nov 13	April 10
1973–4	Oct 17	May 6
1974–5	Sept 29	May 31
1975–6	Oct 8	April 28
1976–7	Oct 30	May 13
1977–8	Nov 17	April 16
1978–9	Nov 16	May 1

After the salad days, winter brings the consolation of crisp nutty celery, hot buttered crumpets by a log fire, home-made soups, tripe and onions, roast chestnuts and jacket potatoes. I know of no better variety of potato than Desiree for yield, flavour and versatility, and it is magnificent baked in its jacket. But we also like Desiree potatoes boiled in their skins. They should be about hen's-egg size, scrubbed, then popped into boiling, salted water for about 20 minutes. The skins are easily peeled at the table.

Winter also brings a crop of seedsmen's catalogues to brighten a few rain-sodden hours. I like to try new varieties and novelties in the vegetable sections, at least as often as plot space and my budget allow, and I am a firm believer in the ultimate value of going for the best possible seed stocks, even though this involves ordering from several different firms.

For example, Marshalls of Wisbech are deservedly famous for their onion sets and shallots. Their Giant Fen Globe sets are specially treated to prevent bolting and always give a uniform crop of large, golden-skinned onions with an appealing mild flavour. The same firm offers a strain of the veteran variety Ailsa Craig, developed as sets for exhibition use, and Brunswick Blood Red, the only red onion set I have come across.

Marshalls have a courteous, helpful way of doing business and an old-fashioned concern that the customer should get the best possible results from their products. Their onion sets are despatched from March through until early April, not willy-nilly but with weather conditions very much in mind. A note from them acknowledging my order for Giant Fen Globe said, 'Please do not get unduly worried if you do not get your sets immediately at the start of the season. In most areas the best results are obtained from April planting.' They were right and, keeping to the detailed instructions printed on the bag the sets came in, I produced a crop that both took prizes and kept the kitchen supplied right through the winter and well into spring.

In November I like to get a few sackfuls of fallen leaves which I stack in a cylinder of wire netting on the plot. Felixstowe has many tree-lined avenues, and the road sweepers are happy to let one help oneself. Leaf mould made this way is an excellent source of humus for Cowpasture's lightish soil. Beech and oak are the preferred subjects, but plane, maple and chestnut are also good, especially in a mixture. It takes a couple of years to make leaf mould but it is well worth the effort because it beats peat as a source of humus and is a close runner-up to compost.

18

A FLAIR FOR HUSBANDRY

With very few exceptions, we do not dress up to tend our Cowpasture plots. We dress down. For several years I used the jacket of my demob suit, which had been patched to the point where a scarecrow would have rejected it as unserviceable, but whose pockets were still strong enough to hold the gardener's assorted debris. Or so I thought.

In 1976, when the jacket was at last interred, I discovered that an inside pocket had split and the threadbare lining held a treasure trove of half-full seed packets, plant labels, a few pre-decimal pennies and a letter from my mother-in-law giving a graphic account of how her cold frame cucumbers had flourished to the point of embarrassment. 'I just can't give them away,' she wrote. 'People these days don't seem to eat more than a few slices of cucumber at a time. Not like the days when I was young when it was tea on the lawn every fine Sunday in summer, and salmon and cucumber always.'

Among the seed packets that had lost themselves in the jacket lining was an unused packet of Primo cabbage, priced 3d, and dated 1953. So in the interests of science and as it was then April, I sowed a row of the 23-year-old seed. But in vain. Nothing happened and, as later that year even the healthiest crops were contending with the great drought, it was probably just as well that the veteran seeds made no attempt to show above ground.

In 1953 Ryders, the St Albans seedsmen, were offering twenty-four packets of 'tested vegetable seeds, enough to grow all the vegetables for a big family', including French and runner beans, early and maincrop peas and twelve packets of hardy annual flower seeds, all for 10s (50p) post free. And a grower at Stapleford Abbotts in Essex was offering thirty carnation plants for 1s 6d (7½p), two 3- to 4-year-old dessert apple trees for 3s 6d (17½p), and six flowering shrubs for 1s 6d.

Derek is one of the exceptions to the generally low level of couture on the Cowpasture plots. He served for many years in the Royal Navy. Now, retired, he keeps his plot shipshape, and apart from rubber boots and seamen's stockings, is always rigged out in office-smart style for work on his 10 rods. But, like many sailors, Derek gives the impression that he's not really at home on his bit of land. His crops do not seem to bulk as much as his neighbours' and his plants sometimes are singled out for attacks by animal hordes. He's a believer in tarred string, stretched round young cabbages and carrots as a deterrent against rabbits. But it does not work. In the summer of 1978 row after row of Derek's crops were damaged while next door Gordon's crops were unscathed. Derek used tarred string, but Gordon had a 50m roll of wire netting round his patch.

Wellington boots are not the best footwear for a day's work on the plot. I find the feet sweat, socks slip, and the treads constantly fill up with caked soil if there's any moisture about. I put the point to Tom, wisest of gardeners, that the ideal footwear for allotment farming had yet to be invented.

'Not so,' he said. 'Get a pair of leather boots and add a pair of ex-Army or Navy gaiters – that'll keep you snug and sweet in all weathers. But make sure you keep your boots clean and feed 'em plenty of wax to keep 'em soft and supple, then the older you get the nicer-natured they'll be.'

So, though my jackets outlive their usefulness on the plot, my boots do not. Tom is one of those countrymen who delights in passing on his techniques of working with nature and in sharing his lifetime's love of all living things. He has taught Margaret and me and our children so much that our debt to him can never be repaid.

I once admired his home-made walking stick and six months later he came over to my plot with one he had made for my use. Cut from a two-year-old ash branch, it was then set to straighten in a jig made of a board with 4in nails at critical points. This was left in his Cowpasture shed for twenty-odd weeks, and another fortnight allowed for sanding down and polishing the handle. Now, I would no more think of taking a walk in the country without my stick than I would without my dogs. It is a useful prop at all times – handy for prodding at puddles, turning brambles aside, waving at people, and stemming the slide down muddy banks – but it is a limb-saver on icy afternoons.

Fine, powdery snow, driven by an east wind, is as penetrating as goose fat. In the blizzard of New Year's Eve 1978 the snow found its way through the slate roof at home and built up into drifts that would have brought down ceilings when the thaw came. When I went to the plot I found the shed half full of snow that had drifted in through the gap round the door.

Tom told me the tip of finding the cracks in the shed's timber by sitting inside with the door tightly shut, then filling the cracks with soft putty or waterproof tape. Smiler, from whom I inherited my plot and who worked wizardry with wood, always tarred the outside of his shed, reckoning that a good coat of tar would last all of ten years. And he had a special technique for removing the grime from antique furniture. First he used neat rhubarb juice to rub off the filth of ages, then to put the natural gloss back into the wood he used a muslin bag of crushed walnut kernels, working the nut oil into the grain of the wood.

In his tiny cottage each piece of furniture was a delight to the nose as well as the eyes. And Smiler made his own wine to a recipe that produced a brew so strong that it would take the paint off a door. In his final few years Smiler had the disconcerting habit of talking of dead relatives and friends as though they were still alive. But, although at turned eighty his mind was slipping into the innocence of childhood, his green fingers still produced some of Cowpasture's finest crops.

151

'See this?' he said, holding out a mammoth snow-white cauliflower. 'This is for my Gran. She's crazed me all week for a cauli to pickle.' Gran, at rest in Walton churchyard, had crazed no one for many a long year, but her presence never left Smiler's thoughts.

Small, rotund, bald and with wide blue eyes in a pink, chubby face, Smiler's appearance belied the stubbornness of his character. In an argument he would never yield even though verbally defeated. And when, in that last year, he came to Cowpasture every day but just stood by his shed looking at his plot as it became a wilderness of weeds, his friends tried gently to bring the reality to him of what was happening. But he would have none of it. The landscape he was watching was not what they saw. It was the plot as it had been fifty or more years before: immaculate, grossly productive, the envy of his friends and neighbours. And his smile was that of a proud young husband and provider.

I wish he could see the plot now because I have done my best to keep alive his flair for fine husbandry. Smiler worked to a routine which, of course, is what farming is all about, and the old saying that the best muck for a farmer's land is the farmer's boots is true also of the allotment plot.

The vegetable garden needs the frequent – preferably daily – attention of the gardener, with a routine built around sowing seeds in season, planting out, gathering crops as needed for the kitchen, and topping up the compost heap. Then there's the checking of wire-netting fences, cloches and cold frames, and the cleaning of any tools used. In autumn there's the daily stint of digging vacant land; in summer the hoe is in daily use.

At least once a week crops are searched for insect pests and the first signs of disease. Weekly in the winter I take a bag of ash saved from the log fires at home and add it to the sack in the shed on my plot. That's a potent feed for next summer's outdoor tomatoes. Twice yearly, when the chimneys are swept, a bag of soot goes to the plot to be weathered for use on the celery and onions.

A monthly task is to check the cropping plan, drawn up in December and modified at the request of the cook or owing to my forgetfulness, and to review the plot's profit and loss account and log the findings so that mistakes are not repeated too often.

Once a year, usually in late summer, the shed is turned out: stored fertiliser and lime, potions and powders are made secure for the winter, the first-aid kit is re-primed with Elastoplast dressings, the roof is checked for weathertightness and the rest is creosoted.

Finally, the Christmas break brings two tasks that round off the gardening year with a foretaste of the future: making a plan for the plot to ensure successful rotation of the brassicas, and the fireside search through the seedsmen's catalogues for the old favourites and the bright newcomers.

If we had a bit more help from the professional weather forecasters some of Cowpasture's calamities could be prevented. But even with an array of sophisticated aids that include computers fed by satellites and weather ships, the Met Office can only hope for a 50 per cent success rate in long-range forecasts – and that, if the truth were known, really means the next fortnight. So I make weather a daily routine, logging the maximum and minimum temperatures, rainfall, wind direction and speed, and barometric pressure – elementary data, but enough for me to be able to add a very local forecast to the regional one issued by the experts.

The only certainty about the weather and gardening is that you must take the chance when it comes because you seldom get a second one. In the tussle with our climate help is always offered by the down-to-earth boffins at the National Vegetable Research Station which was established at Wellesbourne, Warwickshire, in 1949. Like that of Lawrence Hills and his Henry Doubleday Research Association, the work of the people at Wellesbourne is both fundamental and far-reaching and both places give a warm welcome to the enquiring vegetable gardener. NVRS vegetable varieties carry the prefix Avon –

Avoncrisp lettuce and Avonresister parsnip are examples – but I believe the early onions still have the Japanese names from which they are derived.

Among the projects being pursued at NVRS, three should have a big impact on the allotment gardener. They are the successful search for strains of maincrop onion that can be sown in summer for harvesting the following June; the production of varieties of outdoor tomatoes that will give a good crop of ripe fruits even in a dull summer; and the development of pre-germinated seeds.

The cold, wet spring of 1978 proved how difficult it is to ensure even germination with onion, carrot and parsley seeds. At Cowpasture many of us found failure rates of up to 90 per cent with early carrots, and there were some total failures with parsnip and parsley sowings. Now Wellesbourne has come to the rescue with a new planting technique that is simple but extremely successful.

The seeds to be sown are germinated indoors in a warm place using damp felt or blotting paper – like sowing mustard and cress. When the root is about 1/10in long, the seeds are sprinkled in the sowing medium. This is cellulose wallpaper paste, diluted to half the strength recommended for wallpapering. About half a pint is sufficient to sow a 15ft row of carrot seed. Seeds and paste are then put into a clear plastic bag with a small hole cut in the corner and the seed is sown in the drill by squeezing the bag. It's rather like icing a cake. The seeds can be spaced evenly after a bit of trial and error and they certainly get away to a good start, with enough moisture retained in the sowing medium to ensure that they suffer no setback, even in a dry spell after sowing.

So, with new techniques, new varieties and one's own experiments, there is always something to look forward to at Cowpasture and all those other plots where food is hand-grown, from seed sowing to harvesting. And the summer ahead may bring every gardener's dream come true: days filled with warm sunshine and nights with soft rain – who knows?

APPENDIX:
USEFUL ADDRESSES

Organisations

British Naturalists' Association, 43 Warnford Road, Tilehurst, Reading, Berks

Cambridge Plant Breeding Institute, Maris Lane, Cambridge

Conservation Society, 228 London Road, Reading, Berks

Council for the Protection of Rural England, 4 Hobart Place, London SW1W 0HY

Friends of the Earth, 9 Poland Street, London W1

Henry Doubleday Research Association, Bocking, Braintree, Essex

Horticultural Research Station, Cambridge

Men of the Trees, Crawley Down, Crawley, Sussex

National Allotments Society, Drayton House, Gordon Street, London WC1

National Trust, 42 Queen Anne's Gate, London SW1

National Vegetable Research Station, Wellesbourne, Warwickshire

Royal Horticultural Society, Vincent Square, London SW1P 2PE

Royal Society for the Protection of Birds, The Lodge, Sandy, Beds

Scottish Plant Breeding Station, Pentlandfields, Edinburgh

Society for the Promotion of Nature Conservation, The Green, Nettleham, Lincoln

Soil Association, Walnut Tree Manor, Haughley, Stowmarket, Suffolk

Seedsmen

Asmer Seeds Ltd, Leicester

Bees Ltd, Sealand, Chester

Chase Compost-Grown Seeds, Benhall, Saxmundham, Suffolk

Chiltern Seeds, Chesham, Bucks

Dickson, Brown & Tait Ltd, Timperley, Altrincham, Cheshire

Dobie, Samuel, & Son Ltd, Llangollen, Clwyd

Dom Seeds Ltd, Spalding, Lincs

Hurst Gunson Cooper Taber Ltd, Witham, Essex

Johnson, W. W., & Son Ltd, Boston, Lincs

Marshalls, Wisbech, Cambs

McLean, John, & Son, Dornoch Farm, Crieff, Perthshire (seed potatoes)

Robinson, W., & Sons Ltd, Sunnybank, Forton, nr Preston, Lancs

Suttons Seeds Ltd, Torquay TQ2 7QJ

Thompson & Morgan Ltd, Ipswich, Suffolk

Unwins Ltd, Histon, Cambridge

Van Hage, Great Amwell, Ware, Herts

Webbs Garden Seeds Ltd, Sealand, Chester

FURTHER READING

Balfour, E. B., *The Living Soil* (Faber, 1975)
Bartrum, Douglas, *The Gourmet's Garden* (Faber, 1964)
Bell, Adrian, *A Suffolk Harvest* (Bodley Head, 1956)
Bruce, M. E., *Commonsense Compost Making* (Faber, 1967)
Bush, Raymond, *Soft Fruit Growing* (Penguin, 1951)
Chinery, Michael, *The Natural History of the Garden* (Collins, 1977)
Drabble, Phil, *Country Seasons* (Michael Joseph, 1976)
Evans, George Ewart, *The Horse in the Furrow* (Faber, 1960)
Genders, Roy (ed.), *Pears Encyclopaedia of Gardening* (Mayflower, 1975)
Gill, Crispin, *The Countryman's Britain* (David & Charles, 1976)
Gordon, Seton, *Wild Birds in Britain* (Batsford, 1949)
Green, Joyce Coynyngham, *Salmagundi* (J. M. Dent, 1947)
Hills, Laurence D., *Organic Gardening* (Penguin, 1977)
Hopkins, Donald, *Chemicals, Humus and the Soil* (Faber, 1975)
Huxley, Anthony, *Plant and Planet* (Allen Lane, 1975)
Janes, E. R., *The Vegetable Garden* (Penguin, 1954)
Jefferies, Richard, *Field and Hedgerow* (Lutterworth Press, 1948)
Lowe, T. A., *The Craft of the Cottage Garden* (C. Arthur Pearson, 1957)
Macself, A. J. (ed.), *Sanders Encyclopaedia of Gardening* (W. H. & L. Collingridge, 1945)
Meteorological Office, *Course in Elementary Meteorology* (HMSO, 1978)
Ministry of Agriculture, *The Agricultural Climate of England and Wales* (HMSO, 1976)
Mossman, Keith, *The Shell Book of Rural Britain* (David & Charles, 1977)
Palaiseul, Jean, *Grandmother's Secrets* (Penguin, 1976)
Royal Horticultural Society, *The Horticultural Show Handbook* (RHS, 1972)
—— *The Vegetable Garden Displayed* (RHS, 1970)
Russell, Sir John, *World of the Soil* (Fontana, 1970)
Salter, P. J., and Bleasdale, J. K. A., *Know and Grow Vegetables* (Oxford University Press, 1979)
Scarfe, Norman, *The Suffolk Landscape* (Hodder & Stoughton, 1972)
Shewell-Cooper, W. E., *The Complete Vegetable Grower* (Faber, 1973)
Simons, A. J., *The Vegetable Grower's Handbook* (Penguin, 1948, reissued 1977)
Soper, Tony, *Wild Life Begins at Home* (David & Charles, 1975)

INDEX

159

INDEX